Praise for *The Focus Fix*

'A wonderful and convincing book outlining the crucial role that daydreaming plays in our daily lives. In a world full of distraction, the power of daydreaming is vital in creating a relaxed and focused mind. Highly recommended.' STEFAN VAN DER STIGCHEL, PROFESSOR OF COGNITIVE PSYCHOLOGY, UTRECHT UNIVERSITY

'This engaging book brings recent work in psychology and neuroscience to provide clear and easy-to-use ideas about building a life where we have room to dream and to focus. The tips are designed to build creativity, engagement in work, and improve life overall.' HEATHER C LENCH, PROFESSOR OF PSYCHOLOGICAL AND BRAIN SCIENCES, TEXAS A&M UNIVERSITY

'The antidote we've all been seeking. Our overstretched, always-on work culture has left us burned out and confused – unable to see the woods for the trees. *The Focus Fix* posits a real, neuro-backed technique for reclaiming your focus, and achieving success in everything – all while improving your wellbeing and allowing you to take more work breaks.' ADAM NORRIS, CEO, PURE ELECTRIC

'As the world becomes more complex and our attention gets pulled in more directions, the ability to focus and find creative solutions becomes critical. This book offers practical and ⸻ ⸻ ⸻ ⸻ can leverage

immediately to manage and thrive in our ever-changing personal and professional lives.' MATT ABRAHAMS, LECTURER IN ORGANIZATIONAL BEHAVIOUR, STANFORD UNIVERSITY GRADUATE SCHOOL OF BUSINESS

'Brings you to that special place where you can generate truly creative moments by removing life's tensions. It will help bring you to find new moments of discovery and self improvement. Enjoy being creative one day at a time.' DARYL LIM, CO-FOUNDER AND PARTNER, DESIGNTHINKERS ACADEMY SINGAPORE

'Chris Griffiths and Caragh Medlicott hit the mark with this insightful book, targeting the challenges of the attention economy by providing an ejection seat from today's always-on culture – it's a game changer!' SHARON CURRY, CEO, THE TRUSTED EXECUTIVE

'A must-read book of the year. *The Focus Fix* features actionable tips that will skyrocket your career or business to the next level.' NIR BASHAN, AUTHOR OF *THE CREATOR MINDSET*

'A holistic recipe to deal with the stress of the modern world. *The Focus Fix* shows you how to remain human in a world that's going crazy, and how not to behave as a machine or an overwhelmed "busy fool". This book will certainly grab your focus.' ANASTASIA DEDYUKHINA, KEYNOTE SPEAKER, BESTSELLING AUTHOR AND FOUNDER OF CONSCIOUSLY DIGITAL

'Demystifies creativity and helps people not only find clarity and unlock their own creativity, but also apply it to everyday challenges in simple, enjoyable ways.' ALISON JONES, FOUNDER, PRACTICAL INSPIRATION PUBLISHING

'Chris Griffiths' and Caragh Medlicott's thorough treatise on how our minds actually work and their tips and insights for tuning it to work even more effectively should be at the top of your reading list.' DOMINIC ASHLEY-TIMMS, CO-AUTHOR OF *THE ANSWER IS A QUESTION*

'Aids in reimagining our approach to work and education in an era shadowed by AI and automation. Griffiths and Medlicott present a new paradigm shift in understanding focus and transform it into an accessible tool that allows us to effectively manoeuvre through the complexities and demands of the modern world.' DINA FIADI, CONSULTANT, SPEAKER, COACH AND MENTOR

'A timely book. The demands of the attention economy and our battle with techno-stress are huge, current issues.' BILL LOWE, LEADERSHIP AND LEARNING CONSULTANT

'This book forces you to pause and reflect to ensure you don't fall into the traps of being a busy fool! It will give you permission to stop and make space for more creativity and calm in your life and at work.' LIZ OSELAND, COACH, TRAINER AND FACILITATOR

The Focus Fix

*Finding clarity, creativity and resilience
in an overwhelming world*

Chris Griffiths

Caragh Medlicott

First published in Great Britain and the United States in 2024 by Kogan Page Limited

2nd Floor, 45 Gee Street
London
EC1V 3RS
United Kingdom
www.koganpage.com

8 W 38th Street, Suite 902
New York, NY 10018
USA

Kogan Page books are printed on paper from sustainable forests.

© Open Genius Limited, 2024

ISBNs
Hardback   978 1 3986 1612 7
Paperback   978 1 3986 1610 3
Ebook   978 1 3986 1611 0

British Library Cataloguing in Publication Data
A CIP record for this book is available from the British Library.

Library of Congress Cataloging-in-Publication Data
Names: Griffiths, Chris, author. | Medlicott, Caragh, author.
Title: The focus fix : finding clarity, creativity and resilience in an overwhelming world / Chris Griffiths, Caragh Medlicott.
Description: London ; New York, NY : Kogan Page Inc., 2024. | Includes bibliographical references and index.
Identifiers: LCCN 2024014994 (print) | LCCN 2024014995 (ebook) | ISBN 9781398616103 (paperback) | ISBN 9781398616127 (hardback) | ISBN 9781398616110 (ebook)
Subjects: LCSH: Creative ability in business. | Mindfulness (Psychology) | Burn out (Psychology)
Classification: LCC HD53 .G748 2024 (print) | LCC HD53 (ebook) | DDC 650.1–dc23/eng/20240505
LC record available at https://lccn.loc.gov/2024014994
LC ebook record available at https://lccn.loc.gov/2024014995

Typeset by Hong Kong FIVE Workshop, Hong Kong
Print production managed by Jellyfish
Printed and bound by CPI Group (UK) Ltd, Croydon CR0 4YY

CONTENTS

About the authors viii
Acknowledgements xi

Introduction: Boiling frogs 1

1 A surprising way to find focus 14

2 Battling burnout in a connected world 37

3 Unlock your untapped creative potential 57

4 The misinterpreted mental voyage 74

5 Doing less to achieve more 95

6 Reconnect with your curious mind! 119

7 Productive mind wandering 138

8 Harness the power of focused daydreaming 156

9 Escape Busy Fool Syndrome 181

10 Fixing your focus at work 195

11 Soaring swans 215

References 227
Index 242

Additional resources, templates, articles and downloads can be found at ChrisGriffiths.com

ABOUT THE AUTHORS

Chris Griffiths

Chris Griffiths is a bestselling author with decades of experience in the areas of creativity, metacognition and innovation. His books have been published in over 20 languages and his previous title, *The Creative Thinking Handbook*, was selected by *Forbes* as one of the best books to 'get your creative juices flowing' and named the #1 business book for inspiring innovation by *CEO Today*.

Chris is the founder and CEO of OpenGenius, a company focused on transforming thinking, creativity and learning through cutting-edge tools powered by Artificial Intelligence. These tools have already been used by millions of individuals worldwide to help generate game-changing ideas and manage the completion of major projects.

In addition to his role as CEO, Chris is also a keynote speaker who has worked with senior leadership teams at the European Commission, Pfizer, State Bank of India, Stanford University, Medline and many more, inspiring teams to systemize their innovation, foster resilience and find their way to success. Chris has helped Nobel laureates, governments, royal families, CEOs and thousands more.

Chris has contributed articles to publications including *Forbes*, *GQ*, *Harvard Business Review Ascend*, *The Times*, *Director Magazine* and many more. To date, he has authored many articles on the topics of metacognition, burnout, creativity and focused daydreaming.

As we head into a future shadowed by AI and automation, where many tasks are shifted away from humans, Chris Griffiths shows us our path to standing our cognitive ground, to reimagining work and education, and to rethinking the very purpose of human cognition. Find out more about Chris and his work at ChrisGriffiths.com.

Caragh Medlicott

Caragh Medlicott is a full-time freelance writer, author and journalist. After graduating with a first-class BA (Hons) degree in English Literature and master's degree in Creative Writing from Cardiff University, she carved out a career in Marketing and PR, coordinating pieces in publications including *GQ*, *Forbes*, *The Times* and many others.

She has held a number of editorial positions, including serving as Interim Editor of Wales' leading arts and cultural publication, *Wales Arts Review*. She has contributed to a number of podcasts and appeared numerous times on the BBC.

Caragh has collaborated with Chris Griffiths on a number of projects since 2019, co-writing articles on the topics of innovation, creativity and daydreaming, which have appeared in a wide range of publications including *Stylist*, *Elite Business Magazine*, *Belfast Telegraph*, *Irish Tech News*, *Metro* and countless others. She is the co-author of the second edition of *The Creative Thinking Handbook*, written with Chris Griffiths and Melina Costi.

Caragh is also the author of several published short stories. In 2020, she was shortlisted for the Lunate 500

Award, and in 2021 she was selected as a finalist in the '30 Below' competition run by *Narrative* (a San Francisco-based literary magazine). In 2022, she was shortlisted for the Creative Future Writer's Award.

Leveraging a wealth of scientific research and studies, Caragh Medlicott demonstrates the benefits of a new way to find resilience in an overwhelming world – and how to use an everyday tool for sharpening your focus and reaching higher achievement levels.

ACKNOWLEDGEMENTS

Writing this book has been a fascinating and enlightening journey; a journey that would have been significantly more challenging without the contributions and support of others.

A profound thank you to Caragh Medlicott, my co-author, whose genius with words and exceptional research has been an integral part of ensuring this book sees the light of day. It would not have happened without her amazing work.

I am extremely grateful to all the readers of my former book, *The Creative Thinking Handbook*. Your valuable feedback filled many gaps and helped to shape this current title, creating a foundation on which we could build this vital work.

Kudos to the team at OpenGenius for their unremitting support over the past two decades. Our mutual journey towards promoting innovation and creativity has been nothing short of fantastic.

Without the insights from numerous coaches and trainers I've had the pleasure to work with over the years, both within and beyond the OpenGenius network, this book may not be as pragmatic or insightful. Their hands-on perspective to creativity has been priceless.

I also want to acknowledge the efforts of others involved with the book including Ally-Joh Gowan Day, who contributed when deadlines seemed tight, and the amazing team at Kogan Page, especially Matt James, our commissioning editor. Your hard work and belief are deeply appreciated.

Lastly, my deepest appreciation extends to my loving family, whose unfaltering support and love have been the foundation of all my work.

Although writing this book has been a challenging endeavour for Caragh and I, looking back, every effort has been worthwhile. It is our ardent wish that this book goes on to help you – the reader – to unlock your true creative potential, increase productivity, and avoid burnout by adopting the practice of focused daydreaming in order to redefine your approach to work and life. Success is really just around the corner.

Chris Griffiths

Introduction

Boiling frogs

L et's talk about frogs. I'll admit, it may seem a strange way to start a book about focus, but stay with me for a moment.

This particular story comes in the form of a proverbial science experiment. As legend has it, Victorian researchers discovered that a frog would jump out of a boiling pot of water but fail to notice if it was slowly boiled alive (Fallows, 2009). While the scientific validity of this experiment has since come under question, what remains is a startlingly apt metaphor for our current working environment.

Today, we are constantly afflicted by digital noise, both at work and at home. An onslaught of emails, a barrage of notifications, a conveyor belt of video calls. Amidst this chaos, the temperature has gradually risen, the bubbles have started to fizz, and (without our even knowing it) we have reached boiling point.

The slow creep of technology certainly has a lot to answer for, but what's even worse is our mindset (or, rather, our lack of it). Just like those frogs blissfully unaware of the water rising in temperature all around them, the subtle shifts to our working environments have allowed us to discount the need for radical change in not only how we approach work, but in how we *think* about work.

Instead, reactivity has become the name of the game. Over the last few decades, countless new technologies have appeared, and then been thoughtlessly integrated into our daily processes. Certainly, many of these tools have improved the way we work – and back in 2020, we gained a new perspective on just how crucial such tech can be – but we cannot deny the many bad habits that have come along in tandem.

The 24-hour brain

Since the dawn of the modern office, the line between work and downtime has never looked so blurred. In our pockets, we carry devices many times more powerful than the technology that first put man on the moon (Puiu, 2015). Constantly plugged in, our brains now have less and less time to truly switch off.

Even when we're away from our desk this state of affairs continues. Whether it's fielding emails and work messages after hours, or indulging in social media and the vast array of streaming services, our brains are seldom idle. Indeed, these days, boredom looks increasingly like a relic of the past. But don't be fooled – such constant neuro-stimulation comes at a cost. And for many, that price is starting to look extortionate.

Research suggests that almost half of UK workers are close to burnout, and internationally the picture is even more bleak (CEBR, 2023). According to Gallup's State of the Global Workplace report, only one in five people feel engaged at work – and post-pandemic we have become more stressed and unhappy than ever before (Gallup, 2022). Of course, there are a plethora of drivers of such changes, but it is undeniable that brain fog, burnout and overwhelm have all had a big hand in this shift.

So, where are we going wrong? The answer, as is so often the case, is complicated. But there is one mistake that seems particularly foundational to this flawed way of working. In fact, it could perhaps more aptly be described as a chronic condition. A phenomenon sometimes known as 'Busy Fool Syndrome' (BFS).

This increasingly common malady is a direct result of our inability to focus. The modern workplace is characterized by reactivity, and while we may make attempts at task prioritization, we are so often diverted along the way. Instead of productivity, we have unconsciously placed busyness on a pedestal. We have learned to equate feeling harried, overwhelmed and burned out with a sense of accomplishment.

You might think this a reasonable assumption. After all, you don't feel stressed after a day of doing nothing, do you? And so it follows that finishing the day exhausted must indicate that you've been working hard. But here's the problem: there is a difference between working *hard* and working *well*. Like a hamster on a wheel, expended energy does not always equate to distance travelled.

When our work is predominantly centred around fire-fighting – reacting to problems as and when they occur, juggling requests from colleagues and clients – any possibility of being strategic goes out the window. Even being aware of these challenges isn't enough to truly escape the system. After all, how can you be strategic when unanswered emails are chased a mere 24 hours after first being received? The pervasiveness of this way of working ultimately keeps us locked in the system.

Of course, it would be easy to lay all the blame at technology's door. Every one of us is now immensely reachable. Colleagues halfway across the world can check in with each other at a moment's notice. When everyone has competing priorities, having instant and constant access to each other is not always a good thing. Perhaps it's not surprising, then, that the UK is one of many nations to see their productivity growth grind to a halt in the last decade (Office for National Statistics, n.d.)

And still, a bad workman blames their tools, and we must resist the temptation to lay all the blame at technology's door. Ultimately, tech (like any resource) is neutral. It's how we use it that actually matters. Really, this is good news. It means that the current dysfunctional way of working is not inevitable, and there's no reason we can't find a new, more successful model for getting things done. In fact, that's what this book is here to help you do.

Diagnosing BFS

Are you suffering from Busy Fool Syndrome? Check out the symptoms in the table below to find out for yourself. Tick off two or more and it's probably a case of BFS!

BUSY FOOL SYNDROME – SYMPTOMS CHECKLIST

- Reactive communication. Answering emails and messages as and when they arrive.
- Multi-tasking. Hopping between tasks throughout the day and working week.
- Clouded focus. Struggling to concentrate fully on the work in front of you.
- Mindless meetings. Constantly calling or being called into aimless meetings.
- Missing effort. You feel your output does not equal the effort you've been putting in.
- Constantly harried. There is an ongoing nagging feeling that you're forgetting something and your to-do list never seems to get shorter.

The remote reactivity trap

Of course, it is not only the tide of encroaching technology that is to blame for our flawed working culture. From the rise of remote and hybrid work through to the adoption of more flexible working hours, the office-based model we once knew has been seriously shaken up, and in many cases totally supplanted.

A lot of these changes have facilitated a move towards a more personalized way of working, with employees designing their daily routine around their individual preferences. On paper, such shifts have the potential to be empowering for both organizations and individuals. Yet, they have sadly more often bred counter issues – with reactivity taking precedence over strategy.

Instead of offering an opportunity for focused independent work, remote employees have found themselves called into an endless stream of video calls. Those choosing alternative working hours have become dogged by paranoid managers who are worried that without constant check-ins, employees cannot be trusted to stay on-task. Where there may have been an opportunity to forge a new way of working, we have found instead new ways to be overwhelmed and creatively stifled.

Research from Microsoft has shown that, indeed, the number of meetings has increased in the last few years – and even more worryingly that back-to-back video meetings literally cause stress to build up in the brain (Microsoft, 2021). You may also be aware of the 'quiet quitting' phenomenon – a trend that has ostensibly seen an increasing number of employees decide to opt out of doing anything but the bare minimum at work.

Despite the prominent coverage of quiet quitting in the media, there is good reason to suppose that the real problem fuelling trends of this ilk is actually disengagement rather than laziness. In fact, research from Ricoh Europe found that only 4 per cent of workers admitted to doing the bare minimum at work. While, interestingly, the same research found that 64 per cent of workers said that they would find work more enjoyable if they were given time to be creative (Ricoh Europe, 2022).

This would suggest that stifled creativity has been the biggest driver of poor engagement at work. We have been poisoned by a particularly potent cocktail of apathy and distraction – robbing us of focus in our daily working life. If we're to overcome these challenges, we must embrace a new mindset that has the resilience to withstand whatever our fast-changing work environment may throw our way.

The creativity gap

OK, so we can agree that our modern way of working is not conducive to being productive. But that's not the only thing it disrupts. Everyone knows that creativity is a powerful tool when it comes to being successful at work. Often touted as the secret sauce that turns tiny start-ups into FTSE 100 giants, in our myth-making about creativity we have often lost sight of just how fundamental it is to our overall mindset.

Because creativity is much more than a bit of transformational magic reserved for Silicon Valley entrepreneurs. It is a quality and pursuit with enormous everyday value. Forget the grandiose stories of innovative geniuses for a moment, and consider instead that creativity is, actually, a powerful everyday habit which can yield huge benefits when it comes to finding focus.

I have spent the majority of my career busting the persistent myth that creativity is an elusive quality bestowed on a lucky few. That is because this way of thinking has no grounding in fact. Creativity is just a skill like any other, one which can be developed and honed – polished and perfected. That is why I believe passionately that creativity is for everyone. Yes, even you.

But why does it even matter? Well, that's a bigger question. Everything we have ever achieved as a species can be linked back to our propensity for creative thinking. That's why – whether we like it or not – creativity at work matters. It is at once our heritage and our future. It is also likely why there is such a huge and undeniable link between creativity and job satisfaction.

Research has shown that, even in job roles that are not traditionally creative, an engaged creative environment is associated with decreased absenteeism and increased job satisfaction (Mayfield et al, 2020). To be clear, this doesn't apply solely to creative industries, but to being creative within any job regardless of its requirements. Simply put, the opportunity to be creative gives us purpose.

That is why we can't talk about being successful at work without also talking about creativity. While you might think that distraction is the primary villain of finding focus, you should not underestimate the power of its insidious cousin – apathy. It is a dangerous force that can render even the most inspired of go-getters lethargic and unfocused.

Making a mindset

I know what you're thinking. Yes, we can all agree that the current working environment is *not* conducive to achieving good work – but how do we actually go about overcoming it? After all, if you're reading this book, there's good reason to suppose this isn't the first time you've tried to tackle the issue.

These days, finding focus isn't so much a hurdle as a mountain. We may have the depths of the internet at our fingertips, and yet this whirlpool of information often feels more overwhelming than empowering. The truth is, much of what can be found online – from productivity 'hacks' to project management software – focuses on treating symptoms rather than the actual root of the issue. To really treat the cause, we need to address our mindset.

For many, 'mindset' has become little more than a buzzword. The problem with buzzwords is that they become oversaturated and overused so that we lose all perspective on what they actually mean. That's why, in order to change our mindset, we also need to consider what mindset actually *is*.

The Cambridge Dictionary defines mindset as 'a person's way of thinking and their opinions' – and while this is certainly true, it doesn't really do justice to exactly how pivotal mindset can be (Cambridge Dictionary, 2019). In fact, I would argue that when it comes to finding focus – mindset is everything.

In 2005, the National Science Foundation found that the average person has about 12,000 to 60,000 thoughts per day. Of those thoughts, around 80 per cent were deemed negative, and 95 per cent were repeated thoughts from the day before. That's a lot of information flowing through our brains every day. When we start to change those thoughts, we have a huge opportunity to alter our behaviours as well.

That's why I like to think of mindset as a framework – a mental scaffolding from which all our actions are built. Without a purposeful mindset, even well-intentioned efforts run the risk of falling apart. That's why we need to be strategic in fostering a foundational mindset upon which everything else can be built.

Of course, the problem is – like it or not – you already have a mindset. Unlearning bad habits can be as important as establishing new ones. That's why to change our mindset we need to incorporate new ideals and reshape our thinking patterns so that they better reflect the person we'd like to be.

The good news is that this is exactly what this book is here to help you do. This won't be a solely educational pursuit, either, because I have a secret weapon to make finding focus easier than you thought possible. But before we can get into that, we need to look more closely at what focus really means.

The DNA of focus

So, we've defined mindset – but what about focus itself? While focus may seem like a self-evident concept, there are actually lots of facets to its overall DNA. In many ways, our failure to recognize these facets is part of what prevents us from achieving it.

For example, we might think of focus as a form of concentration – the ability to lock into a piece of work or particular subject and so give it our undivided attention. Certainly, it's true that we can understand focus in this way when thinking about it technically. But what's even more important is how we think about it in relation to the everyday.

This is because focus is much more than just the application of attention – it is the ability to consistently give your attention to the right things, and the quality of that attention when it is given. After all, the issue we currently face isn't that we're totally incapable of focusing, but rather that our focus is fissile and flighty. When we flit between various technological tools, constantly stimulating our frontal lobe, we deplete our ability to focus in a real, high-quality way.

Not only this, we actually increase our risk of mental fatigue and ultimately burnout. Add into this picture the fact that everything from social media to email can interfere with our brain chemistry – fuelling our addiction to the high of a continually renewed stream of notifications – and you have an environment that is incredibly hostile to achieving true focus.

In many ways, we humans are simple creatures – we gravitate towards what makes us feel good and attempt to avoid what doesn't. In evolutionary terms, this is a decent system for survival. When it comes to tackling work we might find challenging, mundane or demanding... it's not so great. Especially when we are constantly inundated with options to funnel our attention elsewhere (even when those areas have the guise of productivity – such is the insidious nature of BFS).

Recognizing the incredible power focus has to transform not only how you work, but what you might achieve with that work, is the first step towards fostering it in a meaningful way. Really, focus is like sunshine – whatever is placed beneath its rays has the potential to bloom and grow. In order to get the most from our focus we need to tend the whole garden, as well as the light itself.

The daydream secret

This book will teach you how to change your mindset through a combination of context, education and the application of an actionable tool that can totally rewire your mindset from the inside out. This technique has the power to not only help you find focus, but also to empower you to achieve more while working for less time.

Yes, this may sound like the kind of unrealistic line peddled by a snake oil salesman, but it's actually true. If you don't believe me, then you just have even more reason to give it a try. I can only assume, if you've picked up this book and read this far, that finding focus is something you are pretty serious about (after all, you're giving me your focus right now – and I'm very grateful for it!).

The good news is that this particular technique is effortless. Genuinely. In fact, if you've ever found yourself staring into space or making your commute home on autopilot, then you've likely already done it (and in real terms, there's not a person alive who hasn't). That's because the technique I'd like to recommend to you is daydreaming.

I know, I know. You're reading a book on finding focus and I'm suggesting daydreaming, which is surely the antithesis of focus! You're within your rights to feel that way. In fact, whenever I have shared this suggestion with other business leaders they've often looked at me like I've grown a second head. Well, at least at first. When they put it into practice it's not long before I hear just how transformative it has been for them.

So, while it may seem counterintuitive now, remember that Aristotle once said: 'There is no genius without a touch of madness.' Daydreaming is not something I've made up as a cure for poor focus, but a real, neuroscience-backed technique for enhancing your cognitive capacities.

What's more, I have taken the wealth of scientific research and studies to create a tailored technique which I call 'focused daydreaming' so you can make this tool a real, everyday trick to honing your focus and achieving more. So, while I have your attention – it's time to make this secret work for you.

CHAPTER ONE

A surprising way to find focus

In the chaos of the modern world, finding focus can feel like a daily battle. Our attention is constantly demanded and divided, and there is more technology to distract us from our work than ever before. But I'm here to tell you that if you want to improve your focus, then you need to make more time for being unfocused.

I know how it sounds. When it feels like there are never enough hours in the day, receiving the advice that you should make time for daydreaming can sound at best ridiculous and at worst infuriating. But if there's one thing I hope this book does for you it is to change this perception completely. In fact, if you put the tools suggested here into practice, I'm confident that it will.

We learn early on that daydreaming is something to be avoided – many of us will have been reprimanded at school for looking out of the window or staring into the middle distance. As adults, we often apologize for zoning out of a conversation or activity. The truth is that for most of us, daydreaming is an automatic and involuntary act. Something that happens seemingly by accident, certainly not something we'd ever consider making time or space for on purpose.

But here's the thing. The human brain is both complex and brilliant. Daydreaming isn't a flaw in the system, but a crucial neurological process with a wealth of cognitive benefits. Underestimating daydreaming is much like underestimating sleep – just because you're not directly productive whilst engaging in it, doesn't mean it's not having an impact on your performance elsewhere.

The key difference, of course, is that sleep is not optional. It's something built into all of our routines, and while many of us don't get as much sleep as we would like, no one would suggest we eradicate sleep altogether. Daydreaming is rarely thought of in the same way. In fact, it's rarely thought about at all. This is despite the huge bank of research which clearly demonstrates just how powerful it can be in enhancing our brain function – but before we can get into that, we need to look more closely at our understanding of what daydreaming actually is.

What actually is daydreaming?

How much time have you spent considering the intricacies of the daydreaming process? For most of us, the answer is no time at all. After all, why would you? It is one of the characteristic features of daydreaming that it frequently happens without our conscious say so. You don't think to yourself, 'I'm going to daydream now' – instead, you slip into this state, often without realizing it has occurred until something snaps you from your reverie.

Most of us will have a shared understanding of the word 'daydreaming', but that doesn't mean we have a real grasp of its full meaning, culturally or psychologically. By looking more closely at it through both these lenses, we can really dig into why daydreaming is such an interesting and powerful cognitive phenomenon – one which you can put to use to find more success and focus in your life right now.

Of course, as a term, daydreaming is pretty much self-defining. Sometimes also referred to as 'mind wandering', daydreaming is the act of allowing thoughts to run through your mind in a dream-like fashion whilst awake (hence during the 'day'). While dictionary definitions tend to focus on daydreaming as something characterized by escapism or dissatisfaction with the present moment, experts have actually proposed a multitude of reasons why we sometimes spontaneously shift into the mind-wandering state.

A review in the *Canadian Journal of Experimental Psychology* puts forward five possible functions for daydreaming: 1) Future thinking – an exploratory method for considering how a particular scenario might play out, and what action may need to be taken as a result; 2) Creative thinking – considering multiple perspectives and ideas to produce original creative thought; 3) Attentional cycling – the mind's natural need to vary attention levels in order to sustain overall focus; 4) Dishabituation – a process where a change in routine or environment reawakens you to something which had become invisible or less noticeable to you due to its regular repetition; 5) Relief from boredom – a way to source entertainment in a mundane moment, or motivation while undertaking a boring task (Mooneyham and Schooler, 2013).

There is also more than likely an evolutionary benefit to daydreaming. Mind wandering frequently involves imagining future scenarios (as mentioned above), and this is a trait which would have been very advantageous to our ancestors. After all, living in the moment isn't exactly conducive to anticipating potential threats! Even so, daydreaming is much more than a happy evolutionary accident, it is actually foundational to our neurological functioning. Understanding it better is the first step towards embracing it as a real technique that can be adapted in order to improve the inner workings of your brain.

Of course, outside the theories and definitions of daydreaming lie our associations with it as both a concept and activity. The way we think about mind wandering will naturally be coloured by our personal experience. Perhaps you were dubbed a 'dreamer' as a child and so carry around accusatory, negative associations with the word. Alternatively, you might enjoy daydreaming, relishing the chance to indulge imaginary scenarios or entertain future possibilities when given the opportunity.

Our cultural understanding of daydreaming, too, is varied – neither wholly positive nor wholly negative. Many will think of daydreaming solely as the remit of childish, *Alice in Wonderland*-esque fantasy. Meanwhile, others may connect the act to great breakthroughs, such as the story of Isaac Newton conceiving of gravity after being stirred from a daydream by a falling apple (and there will be more on the mind-wandering greats in Chapter 3!).

Still, whatever your current associations with daydreaming, I must ask that you wipe the slate clean before proceeding any further with this book. The personal and cultural baggage we attach to a particular concept can negatively impact our ability to engage with it wholly and truthfully. In order to really get to grips with daydreaming and its many possibilities, you need to reconnect with it as a technique with the potential to rewire your brain from the inside out.

Under the lid

So, we understand daydreaming as a concept – but what is actually happening inside the brain when our mind goes a-wandering? It's an interesting question, and one with even more interesting results, thanks to a number of scientists who have attempted to tackle it in their research.

While we're often aware of the normal mental shifts that we go through any given day – whether that be moving between sleep and waking, or simply the natural ebb and flow of our mood – our brain continues to run expertly and continuously in the background. Whether we're privy to it or not, the quality of these neurological processes can have a big impact on our behaviour and perhaps, more importantly, on our focus.

Luckily for us, a number of scientific studies have already taken a look inside the human brain so that we can see and understand exactly what's happening under the lid when we daydream. Spoiler alert: it's not just tumbleweeds blowing around in there!

One such study was undertaken by the University of British Columbia (UBC) in 2009, and this played a huge role in changing perceptions of daydreaming from a neuroscience perspective – reshaping our understanding of its cognitive purpose and role. Led by Professor Kalina Christoff, the researchers from UBC set out to understand what was going on inside the brain during periods of mind wandering, placing subjects inside fMRI scanners (a brain imaging tool) and having them perform simple routine tasks – live tracking their attentiveness, as well as their performance on the assigned tasks (Christoff et al, 2009).

While the researchers had expected to see a decrease in brain activity during periods of inattentiveness, they soon discovered this was not the case. Instead, their results showed that the brain's default network (associated with easy, routine and introspective mental activity) was not the only part of the brain active during daydreaming sessions as had first been predicted. Instead, their results indicated that the executive network (associated with high-level, complex problem solving) also lit up during periods of mind wandering.

The study ultimately concluded that daydreaming is an important cognitive state which may play a crucial role in not only creative thinking, but also in problem solving (as indicated by the activity detected in the brain's executive region). This, of course, completely disrupts our surface-level perception of daydreaming as a form of unproductive, circuitous mental play. Instead, it suggests that the periods of inattentiveness we all experience are actually crucial to our ability to find solutions to complex problems in daily life.

This research also suggests that – from a cognitive perspective – the focused and unfocused minds operate in very different ways. During periods of concentration, we can think of our focus as spotlight – other parts of the brain power down to allow our attention to be intensified, highlighting what's in front of us. By contrast, the daydreaming mind is like a soft ambient glow, allowing other areas of the brain to connect in ways that simply aren't possible when we're using our full attention.

In many ways, we are like the devices we use day in day out; the longer we're switched on, the quicker we run out of battery. Of course, many of us will have experienced this anecdotally in our own lives. After a long day of work, it is not unusual to feel that our brain is fried or worn out. The irony is, we're much more likely to push on with work when we're facing problems, than when things are going well. Yet, the above research from UBC suggests this might actually be the worst thing we can do – with innovative solutions much more likely to bud and grow in the soft, connective light of the unfocused brain.

Of course, this fact is perhaps not as surprising as it may seem. Ask people where they get their best ideas, and you rarely hear 'at my desk' or 'in a meeting' – instead, inspiration seems to strike at random and even inopportune moments. No wonder common visualizations depict creativity as a light bulb turning on or a bolt of lightning from on high.

Here are just a few of the answers I regularly receive when I ask people where their best ideas hit them: in the bath or shower; commuting to or from work; out on a run or a walk; falling asleep or waking up; cooking, washing up or doing other chores; idling or relaxing on a lazy day. Of course, the one thing that connects all these activities is that they are moments primed for daydreaming. Given the above research, we now know this is far from coincidental.

Creativity – a skill, not a trait

Creativity is one of the most coveted qualities in the world. You only need to look at the World Economic Forum's 'The Future of Jobs' report to see evidence of this – with 'creative thinking' ranked alongside 'analytical thinking' as the top skills for workers of the future (World Economic Forum, 2023). That's not to mention that of the 50,000 'most needed' professional skills outlined by LinkedIn, creativity is positioned at number one (Petrone, 2018).

But creativity is more than just a pathway to success – it gives us a sense of purpose and joy in our work. When we're able to utilize creativity in our daily tasks we feel more connected to the importance of what we do. It also improves the quality of our work in more indirect ways. While you might associate creativity solely with idea generation, true creativity can also inspire you to rethink your routine and overhaul your work processes. Inspired action and strategic insight are just a few of the less-talked-about benefits of being a creative thinker.

In this way – and many others – creativity naturally lends itself to enhanced focus. It allows us to better enjoy the work we do, and engage with it in novel, innovative ways. Needless to say, this is something we could all do with a little more of in our working lives. Yet, so many of us think of our creative ability as fixed, and even for those who don't, finding a strategy to actually boost creativity can be daunting.

It's important to note that creativity is not a mystical trait bestowed on us by the muses. Instead, it is something we can train and strengthen through both practice and use. I often find that an erroneous perception of creativity as some elusive talent is what keeps people from making more time for it. That's why it's so important to emphasize that there is no good evidence to suggest creativity is something we inherit genetically.

However, scientists have been able to uncover certain genetic traits that might indicate a propensity for creativity. One such trait is brain plasticity – this refers to the brain's ability to grow and organize its neural networks. This plasticity can be linked to creativity because it is what enables us to learn and grow (and our ability to adapt to change is a fundamental part of innovation).

One genome-wide study published in the National Library of Medicine did find that an increased presence of particular gene clusters may heighten a person's brain plasticity, but what is telling is that this genetic trait does nothing to guarantee creativity as a result (Ukkola-Vuoti et al, 2013). Meanwhile, another scientific study found some evidence that duplicate DNA strands can be tied to serotonin-producing genes (Kraus et al, 2014). This is significant because serotonin (a neurotransmitter) increases connectivity in the brain, improving awareness, perceptiveness and internal thought. Still, neither study was able to make a compelling case for creativity as a primarily biological trait.

In other words, in the instances of both of these studies, the genetic traits explored can go some way in indicating creative potential, but do nothing at all to guarantee it. Equally, when we consider the many creative geniuses to have walked the Earth, the chances that all of them possessed these genetic traits are practically impossible. The learning to take from this is that creativity is not like being able to roll your tongue – something you either can or can't do – but a complex characteristic that can just as easily be nurtured through our actions.

Indeed, the research on techniques that can be employed to boost creativity is plentiful and persuasive. Everything from curiosity to regular walks can have an impact on your creative ability (Weir, 2022). Still, the most overlooked creative technique of them all has to be mind wandering. While other science-backed recommendations are certainly helpful, daydreaming is easy to practise and highly repeatable – allowing you to access the subconscious mind where ideas brew and develop.

Ultimately, daydreaming organically increases our propensity for creative thought, while simultaneously facilitating recuperation time for our overworked brains.

The problem is, in our fast-paced environment, we're doing less and less of it.

The great variety of our brains

That we are all different is one of the truly wonderful things about being human. Everyone has a unique perspective based on their own experiences. Naturally, this means our brains are also different. Even so, creativity is one trait that is native to humans more broadly. The very fact we daydream in the first place – that we're capable of imagining things that haven't happened – speaks to our inherently creative nature. This applies equally to neurotypical brains as it does to neurodivergent ones.

But what is neurodivergence? It's a term you may have heard before – and indeed something that, on a cultural level, we are becoming more aware of in general. In the simplest of terms, our neurological 'make up' refers to different brains' different ways of arranging and/or processing information. The average person has certain commonalities in their neurological make up, which is why we refer to them as 'neurotypical'. For some, however, their mental processing falls outside these parameters in such a way they might be classed as 'neurodivergent' (ND).

The term 'neurodivergent' is an umbrella term, usually used in a non-medical sense, that describes individuals with variation in their mental functions (Gregory, 2022). People with neurological conditions such as Autism Spectrum Disorder (ASD) are considered neurodivergent, as well as people with any developmental condition, such as Attention Deficit Hyperactivity Disorder (ADHD) and Obsessive-Compulsive Disorder (OCD). Quite simply, neurotypical people process information in similar ways, whereas neurodivergent people may process it in other ways, which may lead to notable differences in learning or working styles.

The concept of neurodivergence is attributed to sociologist Judy Singer who, in 1990, challenged the conventional ideas surrounding what is considered to be 'normal' and 'abnormal' cognitively. As someone with ASD herself, Singer was aware of just how different each brain can be and how everyone has a unique set of abilities and needs. Singer's aim, then, was to explain how neurodiversity offered society an opportunity to learn about the people whose brains function differently, and the value they also brought to society.

However, despite the obvious positivity with which Singer approached the topic of neurodiversity, this enthusiasm was sadly not always reflected by others at the time. Often, neurodivergent individuals were underrepresented and very much misunderstood in the media, with their neurological differences seen as a limitation rather than an opportunity for variety and nuance.

Unfortunately, neurodivergent individuals are still sometimes misunderstood. Yet the reality is, when ND individuals experience challenges in one area it almost always allows for extra insight in another. For example, an individual with dyslexia may have issues with text when reading and writing, but the neurological difference that produces this effect is the same difference that makes that same dyslexic individual better at spotting patterns (Medlicott, 2022).

Similarly to neurotypical individuals, neurodivergent individuals are also in danger of burnout and the always-on Busy Fool Syndrome (BFS) way of working in today's culture can be even more limiting and harmful to neuro-divergent individuals.

For example, work is typically completed within certain hours of the day, with 9 am–5 pm still in place as the most dominant office model. This basic timeframe might work well enough for neurotypical individuals, but a set amount of allocated working hours can be much more challenging for neurodivergent individuals. Those with conditions such as ADHD work in short bursts of energy and, due to the intensity of this short-burst work, within this time they can often achieve as much as a neurotypical person might throughout a typical working day. Set working patterns can be harmful to ND individuals and can lead to burnout, so it is important that changes be made in the work environment, such as flexible hours, to improve the quality of work for ND individuals. Of course, with flexible hours should also come the inclusion of regular breaks and the option to work at a pace that suits each individual, rather than mindlessly accepting that constant busyness is the route to success.

Just as there is no 'right' or 'wrong' way for our brains to operate, there is no 'right' or 'wrong' way to be creative either, and it is certainly interesting to consider the different ways a brain can think creatively, especially in the case of ND individuals. More specifically, it is interesting to note the differences in the process of daydreaming in those who are neurodivergent. For example, Ingela Visuri studied how individuals with ASD daydream, noting that they were less constrained by social norms. Individuals who took part in Visuri's study reported that by daydreaming – allowing themselves to partake in imaginary experiences – they were able to get creative and process information in a private mental space removed from societal expectations (West et al, 2022). Individuals with ASD felt that, by daydreaming and existing in imaginary experiences, they could practise their creativity more freely without being concerned about the pressure of real interactions. Studies have also found that individuals with ASD can produce ideas that are, on average, more original and unique than neurotypical individuals. Of course, neurotypical people can similarly uncover more creative ideas by moving beyond the limitations of social expectation.

In fact, individuals with ASD were further proven to come up with more novel, creative ideas than neurotypical individuals with the Alternate Uses Test, which asks participants to come up with as many unusual uses as they can for everyday objects, such as a paperclip (West et al, 2022). Individuals with ASD excelled at converging many different ideas into one theme or pattern, known as convergent thinking. It was also speculated that individuals with ASD rely less on semantic associations so, when it came to participating in the Alternate Uses Test, they could produce more original and novel ideas. Of course, individuals with ASD are just a part of the neurodivergent community, but the takeaway message is still clear: everyone's brain is wonderfully different and capable of wonderfully different ideas. The more differently we look at things, the better we can come together to create novel ideas and inspire each other.

Bored of boredom

When was the last time you felt bored? For many of us, boredom is something we experienced most prominently during adolescence and childhood. Stuck inside on a rainy day, for example, or languishing throughout the endless summer break. While we may have resented these dreary periods back then, there's good evidence to suggest these times were actually crucial to the development of our brain and creative ability (Bench and Lench, 2013).

Of course, boredom is something we still occasionally experience in adulthood. Or at least it used to be. As already touched upon in the introduction, our current culture is replete with not only technological devices but options for constant entertainment. Moments that might once have ushered in the slow creep of boredom – simple activities like standing in line at a shop or walking round the corner – today have become increasingly scarce.

Between podcasts, audiobooks and music, there are endless options to fill every second with ceaseless noise. Whether it's our commute to work or doing the washing up, there is no longer an obligation to be alone with our thoughts. The problem is that being constantly entertained – from a neurological perspective – is pretty similar to being constantly engaged. Without the prompt of boredom, we have much less reason to enter the daydreaming state.

Today, when waiting in a queue, we don't stare idly off into the distance but peruse our phones – enabled to do anything we feel like, whether that be shooting off emails or scrolling social media. Where once there may have been 'nothing to watch on the telly', we now have access to a suite of streaming services with millions of films and TV shows available at all times of the day and night.

And it's not just the entertainment economy driving these changes. Tech has also improved the efficiency of daily life – today you are much less likely to be left on hold for hours at a time, with customer service often available via live chat 24/7 thanks to the rise of Artificial Intelligence (AI) (and there will be more on the implications of AI later). When you need to check a fact or the definition of a word, you don't need to dust off a dictionary or encyclopedia anymore, you can simply access a search engine and find the answer you're looking for within just a few seconds.

On the surface, all of these changes sound like good things. Our lives have become easier, and our options for both information and entertainment more plentiful. The problem of course isn't the benefits – of which there are many – but the way it has altered our overall behaviour. The social and cultural conditions of modern life are sadly robbing us of organic opportunities for daydreaming.

You and the attention economy

It won't surprise you to hear that today, our attention is an extremely valuable resource. And it's valuable not only to us as individuals, but also to the numerous tech companies jockeying to win our focus. These days we are not merely 'customers' but 'users'. This shift has led to the rise of the 'attention economy' – supplanting the 'information economy' which existed before it – with many more demands on our attention than we could ever possibly entertain.

DEFINITION OF THE ATTENTION ECONOMY

'The attention economy is the collective human capacity to engage with the many elements in our environments that demand mental focus. The term reflects an acknowledgement that the human capacity for attention is limited and that the content and events vying for that attention far exceed that capacity.'

Definition taken from WhatIs.com (Wigmore, nd).

As a term, 'attention economy' was first coined by psychologist, economist and Nobel Laureate Herbert A. Simon. He observed that when information is abundant, our attention is the resource that becomes most scarce (and hence valuable). As he puts it: 'A wealth of information creates a poverty of attention' (Hyland, 2023).

Is it any wonder people are struggling to find focus, when an entire economy has been founded on the race to divert and syphon off our attention? So many of us have become addicted to the salve of constant connection and amusement facilitated by technology. This inevitably interferes with our emotional regulation, which is a key part of our ability to find motivation, stay on task, and ultimately produce good work.

It doesn't help, of course, that our device use is almost entirely integrated with our day-to-day life, with one survey finding that 89 per cent of Americans check their phone within the first 10 minutes of waking up (Wheelwright, 2022). Throughout the day, the average person will check their phone a further 85 times (Andrews et al, 2015). This is far from ideal behaviour when you consider it takes roughly 23 minutes for a person to refocus every time they are distracted (Mark, Gudith and Klocke, 2008).

While we may tend to think of willpower and motivation as abilities within our control, they are actually complicated qualities that can be actively curtailed by the proliferation of devices present in our daily lives. Over time, we have become conditioned to feel excited when we hear our phones ping (Duke and Montag, 2017). And it doesn't end with just notifications – even having our phone within view can worsen our ability to get stuff done.

A study published in the University of Chicago Press undertook two experiments to measure how our concentration is influenced by the presence of a smartphone. With a sample size of nearly 800 people, participants were asked to perform tasks that measured cognitive capacity – with some people asked to place their phones in close proximity to themselves (for example, face-down on the desk) and others asked to put their phones out of sight in a bag or another room. The results were decisive – participants with their phones in clear view performed worse on the given tasks (Duke et al, 2018).

Of course, it's important that we understand the context of what we're up against – but do not be disheartened. Knowing the many ways in which the current attention economy can impede our focus can also relieve us of some of the guilt that frequently worsens the vicious cycle of procrastination. The other good news, of course, is that when used correctly daydreaming can offer an ejection seat-style escape from the current always-on culture that keeps us locked into Busy Fool Syndrome (BFS).

Focusing on the solution

'Focused' daydreaming probably sounds like something of an oxymoron. How can you be intentional and focused whilst engaging in something that requires your mind to wander freely? Well, as strange as it may sound on first encounter, 'focused daydreaming' is the term I have developed to describe the technique I believe has the power to help you achieve clarity, creativity and success at work.

I will cover at length the specifics of what focused daydreaming is, and how it can be applied to retrain your brain. But, before we proceed any further, please allow me to briefly outline the basics of this technique and the theory that sits behind it.

I've picked the term 'focused' to indicate that this is a technique that should be applied specifically, but also to refer to the process of gathering information to hone the creative energy of your daydreaming sessions (more on this later). While daydreaming certainly has its benefits as a naturally occurring cognitive phenomenon, to really reap those benefits in a meaningful way we need to bring purpose into the overall process.

Our daydreaming mind is an idea incubator. But in order to focus this creative energy, we need to give our subconscious some dots to join. There are a number of ways of doing this, and those different methods will really depend on what you're working on, and what your overall goal is. For example, on an average workday, taking a few brief, pre-planned focused daydream breaks might be enough to keep your creative momentum going. Alternatively, when working on a big creative project or combatting a particularly thorny problem, more legwork may be required.

Let's go back to that incubator metaphor for a second. Your daydreaming mind can shine the warm light required to grow your best ideas, but if you're not being specific with the seeds you plant don't be surprised if the flowers that bloom are ultimately random and varied. I know what you're thinking: but how can I control what ideas come to me? And while there will always be an extent to which you can't, there is at least a way to influence the direction of your creative mind. We do this through the information we consume and engage with.

You can sort of think of this as sourcing inspiration – the only difference is you shouldn't worry about being hit with ideas during the process. Instead, this presents a way of loading up your subconscious mind with the details of the area you're looking to get creative in. That might mean reacquainting yourself with all the specifics of a challenge you're facing, doing some competitor research, or even creating a mood board.

The basics of the focused daydreaming process can be boiled down to the following three steps:

1 Find your focus. For your daydream session to be productive, you should have an intention in mind. That

might be to uncover ideas for a new campaign or find a solution to a tricky problem – either way, know your desired outcome.

2 Information for inspiration. With your area of focus decided, immerse yourself in this subject – this will fuel and focus the subconscious mind, providing inspiration for breakthroughs when daydreaming.

3 Activate the daydream state. Enter the daydreaming state via your preferred technique (suggested techniques to come later on). When ideas naturally occur, capture them and walk away armed with innovative solutions and recharged mental batteries.

While we'll cover the details of how frequently you should schedule in focused daydreaming sessions and the best way to enter the daydreaming state later on, what's important to know now is that this is an incredibly simple technique that has real power to address the issues outlined in the next chapter. Ultimately, focused daydreaming is like a factory reset for the brain, restoring clarity and clearing the way for both daily and big picture success.

Summary: embracing daydreaming to foster focus and creativity

We have learned daydreaming, an often-underestimated natural cognitive process, can play a pivotal role in enhancing our brain function. While it's considered a habit to avoid, the cognitive benefits associated with daydreaming give it a similar importance to that of proper sleep. Both sleep and daydreaming are fundamental neurological processes essential for rest and increased productivity. Like sleep, daydreaming should not be seen as optional, but built into our routines as something steadfastly important.

Daydreaming allows thoughts to run freely in our minds, often without our conscious control. There are a number of possible benefits to its existence, as it gives us time for future and creative thinking, attentional cycling and relief from boredom. It also has benefits from an evolutionary perspective as it involves imagining future scenarios, something which would have proved advantageous to our ancestors.

It's also essential to understand what happens inside our brains when we daydream. Scientific studies demonstrate that during a daydreaming session, not only is the brain's default network (associated with routine mental activity) activated, but also the regions associated with problem solving. It seems, then, that daydreaming might play a more important role, not only in idea generation but in also finding solutions.

Creativity, a quality intrinsically linked with daydreaming and the key skill of the future, is not merely an inherited trait. It's a complex characteristic that can be nurtured through actions, including daydreaming itself. Given the high demand for creative thinking in today's bustling world, daydreaming can prove an effective tool to boost creativity and focus.

However, the increasing technological advancements and the rise of the attention economy demand continuous engagement, limiting opportunities for organic daydreaming. Our devices keep us perpetually connected and entertained, creating a constant need to shift and divide our focus without natural respite. As a result, we lose the precious and naturally occurring opportunities to daydream, indicating an urgent need to deviate from today's always-on culture.

And so, we put forward 'focused' daydreaming as a suggested technique to redirect our focus and deal with the information overflow. This tool involves having a specific intention, immersing oneself in that subject, and activating the daydream state in order to get creative. This process not only enriches our subconscious minds with details of the area we seek to creatively explore but also helps generate innovative solutions by allowing the whole of our brain to light up and connect in an ambient, daydreaming glow!

CHAPTER TWO

Battling burnout in a connected world

When was the last time you felt truly removed from the trials and tribulations of your day-to-day life? If I asked a few decades ago, you might have given a couple of different answers. Perhaps you'd have mentioned your last holiday. Or a time you escaped to the beach or countryside. Of course, you might still give similar answers today – the key difference now is the sense of removal we're actually capable of achieving (or, more aptly, not achieving) when taking time away from our work.

The rise of the internet – and the many devices we can now access it from – has both empowered and debilitated us. It is hard, in our current moment, to remember a time when we weren't all so connected. And yet, it wasn't so long ago that the constant access to both information and other people we now take for granted was far from commonplace. Indeed, such advancements have not only dramatically altered the pace at which we live our lives, but also the very fabric of our neurology.

These seismic technological shifts certainly go some way in illuminating the position we currently find ourselves in. Speak to almost any colleague or acquaintance and you'll see that finding and maintaining focus is a near-ubiquitous issue, while the recorded levels of stress and burnout continue to rise globally (Gallup, 2023).

So, allow me to take you back, for a moment, to a time before the proliferation of internet access and our always-handy devices. After all, it is only in looking back that we can really appreciate just how much things have changed. Once upon a time, we got by without the whole world in our pockets, and the ability to access anyone, anywhere, no matter how far away, was something reserved for sci-fi visions of the future.

In this period, pre-internet and smartphones, maps were the only way to plot a route to somewhere new – and the best way to reach someone was to pick up the phone and hope that they were in. While such memories may still stir a touch of nostalgia in some of us today, very few would choose to return to these times. The world as it is now is infinitely more convenient and connected.

Back then, our ability to reach others was often pre-carious and routine dependent. So many of the tasks we can now perform at the touch of a button once required a higher dose of intention and dedication. Without search engines, acquainting yourself with a new subject required sourcing a book or enrolling in a class; staying in touch with a friend living abroad was a lengthy game of letter writing and time-zone coordination. In many ways, this era demanded more from us in terms of foresight and attention.

You'd certainly be forgiven for thinking that, as these things have become easier, we'd naturally free up brain space for more important stuff. But – as you'll more than likely be aware – this has not been the case. The reasons for this are manifold, but one key element has been a tendency towards reactivity in the workplace.

The driving mind

When you boil it all down, we human beings are a reactive species. Nobel Prize-winning psychologist Daniel Kahneman, author of *Thinking, Fast and Slow*, posits that there are two key cognitive systems that drive our thinking and the way we go about making decisions.

The first system (System 1) is instinctual, emotional and fast. Conversely, the second system (System 2), is more strategic and methodical in its workings ('slow', in other words). While we are capable of thinking with both systems – and indeed, should ideally aim to gear our brains towards the second system when at work – inevitably, we often fall back on the trappings of System 1 (Kahneman, 2011).

Nowhere is this clearer than in the ways in which technology has entered the modern working world. Instead of making our work more efficient and communication more timely, most of us now feel more stressed and overwhelmed than we ever have done before. But this was not the inevitable outcome of technological upheaval. Taking a lay of the land, it seems we have unwittingly made a rod for our own backs by allowing technology to add to our mental burden rather than relieve it – but the good news is that being aware of the conditions that have led to this is the first step towards changing it.

Of course, all this is not to say that the reactive workings of System 1 are completely or inherently bad – instead, this system works as something of a shortcut drive for the brain. System 1 allows us to conserve mental energy when dealing with familiar patterns, and to react efficiently when faced with a situation that demands action rather than thought (you don't want to be in a methodical frame of mind when deciding how to handle the information that a car is hurtling towards you).

Still, most of us identify more closely with System 2 – the reasoned self who can take time to reflect and consider before taking action. This is despite the fact we are, in all honesty, more often operating from within System 1. When we look at the multiple shifts to the working environment that have occurred in recent times, we can see how System 1 has predominantly coloured our adoption of tech in the workplace. New technological tools have entered the fray, and instead of strategically planning for how they might fit into the bigger picture, we have thoughtlessly added them into the increasingly intoxicating cocktail of tools and standard work processes. It perhaps goes without saying, but the downside of this way of working is the huge uptick of stress and burnout we experience in our daily lives. This not only matters on a personal, wellbeing level, but actually also causes companies to haemorrhage their over-all productive output. In other words, it is in everyone's interest that we change this state of affairs and find a way to restore the balance we have lost in today's working environment.

Multi-app mayhem

Technology has fragmented our work to an unhelpful degree. Every aspect of our work – from communication to task management – is spread across a wide range of applications, accessible via a number of devices. This inevitably causes more overwhelm. Instead of seeing our projects clearly, and having distinct boundaries between when work begins and ends, we are cast adrift in a swirling vortex of constant notifications and competing demands.

In the tumultuous sphere of the modern digital world, individuals are often compelled to resort to multiple applications to carry out their work efficiently. At first glance, this approach appears to be effective; learning to utilize an application intended for a specific task seems reasonably straightforward. However, as the volume of applications in use escalates, the dispersion of information across different platforms also increases, often resulting in the loss of valuable context. The interwoven complexities of integrating these varied applications further exacerbate the situation, ironically complicating life rather than simplifying it.

Intriguingly, these technological solutions, originally conceived to enhance productivity, have surfaced as overwhelming obstacles for many. Instead of providing a focused path towards completing meaningful tasks, these tools often end up dictating a jumbled trail of minor tasks, irrespective of their pertinence to the main goal.

To counter this prevalent issue of multi-app overload, at OpenGenius, we developed Ayoa.com, which is now used by millions of teams and individuals worldwide. Ayoa is an all-in-one personal and team productivity tool and our aim was to amalgamate features of creative thinking, task and project management, collaboration, document writing and presentation delivery into a single, consolidated app. This unique consolidation ensures that information retains its contextual form and relevance, thereby considerably reducing the perplexing dance of multi-app switching.

Research has consistently suggested that constant oscillation between diverse applications – referred to as task switching – is detrimental to productivity, often leading to an uptick in errors and a drop in efficiency. By using Ayoa, individuals can mitigate the perils of task switching, sharpen their focus on the tasks that matter most, and ultimately navigate their way out of the labyrinthine world of multi-app mayhem.

The rise of technostress

You don't need me to tell you what stress is. It is the sensation that the walls are closing in – of there being more demands than you could possibly meet in the timeframe you have. In this sense, stress is a feeling of scarcity. The concern that you don't have enough energy to give to all that is required of you, and that the consequences of this lack of time or ability will result in adverse circumstances.

Stress is a natural human response to difficult situations, and it is certainly not only limited to the realm of work. We might feel stressed when we have many things unfolding in our personal lives, or when our mental energy has become depleted by a number of demanding situations. It can also come in different intensities – the stress we experience when trying to cook a complicated meal, for example, is very different to the stress of a pressing deadline for an important project.

Despite the many shades and varieties of stress, more often than not, the different causes combine together to induce a general sense of overwhelm. This can make tackling the overall sense of stress difficult as there are a number of situations requiring resolution in order for an equilibrium to be restored. After all, when many plates are spinning, it only takes one dish going off-kilter for the whole thing to veer towards collapse.

Writing in the *New Yorker*, Cal Newport puts forward the idea of 'Slow Productivity' – proposing that more strategy is needed in order to confront the onslaught of information which characterizes the modern working day. Newport paints a familiar picture of workplace dysfunction:

> When there's too much for us to imagine actually
> completing, we short-circuit our executive functioning
> mechanisms, resulting in a feeling of anxious unease [...]
> the combined impact of all of the corresponding meetings
> and messages can take over most of your schedule, creating
> an overhead spiral of sorts in which you spend significantly

more time talking about work than actually getting it done – a form of wheel-spinning freneticism that amplifies frustration and, ultimately, leads to burnout.' (Newport, 2022)

Today, this sensation of generalized overwhelm has only been heightened by technology. Integrated as it is with all areas of our life, our many tech tools have become like oil in the machinery – except, instead of allowing the machine to run more efficiently, the cogs have started to spin at an increasingly unsustainable rate. As more technology enters the picture, our ability to adapt to it in a healthy way becomes ever more impeded. This phenomenon is so prevalent it even has its own name: 'Technostress'.

The concept of technostress was first popularized by psychologist Craig Brod in the 1980s. While Brod could not have anticipated just how prevalent and all-consuming technology would become in the next couple of decades, the definition provided in his book *Technostress* still provides a useful starting point for understanding this condition. He defines it thus: '[The] modern disease of adaptation caused by an inability to cope with the new computer technologies in a healthy manner' (Brod, 1984).

That word 'healthy' is key here – while many of us are entirely proficient as users of technology, we frequently struggle to maintain a healthy relationship with the tools we utilize on a daily basis. Technostress – including its triggers and causes – can be best sorted into the following categories (Sharma, 2023):

Techno-overload

Techno-overload occurs most commonly when a task or project demands the use of multiple technologies, tools or applications in order to be completed. This, in turn, leads to information being dispersed across channels and frequently adds to a sense of overwhelm. This state of techno-overload is especially characterized by a high volume of technology-based communication (whether that be email, instant messaging, video calls or a mix of all these mediums and more). The result is a sense of over-stimulation and stress that causes those afflicted to feel that technology is actually making it harder, or more challenging, for them to reach their desired end goal.

Techno-invasion

Techno-invasion is characterized by the expectation that employees and teams must be constantly connected via technology. A good example of this is when employees are expected to reply to emails or work messages out of hours, or even when this expectation is not officially stated, that the company culture is such that an implicit pressure to always be reachable leads to the same outcome. The word 'invasion' is evocative here, indicating the sensation that work (via tech channels) has infiltrated parts of a person's life which would usually be kept distinct from their job.

Techno-complexity

Techno-complexity most often occurs when a person feels that in order to do the work required of them, they need to continually build or relearn new technological skills. While, of course, upskilling in such a way can be a positive thing, what makes techno-complexity distinct is the stress the demand to use new tools creates, by, for example, causing fear or confusion in the individual. Ultimately, this creates a toxic situation in which the individual is more worried about adapting to technologies than actually doing their work.

Techno-uncertainty

Techno-uncertainty is most commonly seen in companies where a fast-paced environment means that there is a continual influx of digital transformation. This creates a culture where ongoing technological adaption is required – much in the same way it is with techno-complexity. However, the key difference here is that these technological shifts can lead to uncertainty amongst workers, who may never quite feel abreast with the variety of applications and tools used. This problem may be spotlighted by difficulty onboarding new employees, or in maintaining access to certain tools when long-serving employees leave.

Techno-insecurity

Last, but certainly not least, is techno-insecurity. This form of technostress occurs when an individual or team is worried that their job will be either partially or entirely replaced by advancements in technology. With recent advancements in AI, this particular form of technostress has become only more pressing and pertinent for many workers. It is also one of the key reasons it's important we're able to move away from stress and overwhelm so that we can instead maximize our propensity for creative thinking – a skill that distinguishes humans from AI tools.

The melted candle

While in an ideal world we would always have the perfect work-life balance, there are inevitably occasions where extra effort is required of us. This isn't, in itself, a huge issue. Most of us will experience quieter periods at work, as well as busy ones, and this enables us to rest and recuperate – replenishing our energy stores – so we can give our all when going through a more demanding period.

The trouble is, those quieter working times are becoming increasingly rare, and the quality of the downtime we do actually get is often compromised by our problematic approach to work, and the broader culture that surrounds it. In other words, the chronic state of BFS in the workplace is causing our mental energy to become depleted – and that ultimately leads to one thing: burnout.

Of course, you're more than likely already familiar with the concept of burnout. It's even something we've already touched upon in this book. Burnout has certainly become something of a buzzword in recent years – and like all buzzwords, we have found ourselves somewhat removed from the real definition that sits behind the term. So, let's dive a little more into what burnout actually is and why it's such a pressing issue in our current working moment.

What is burnout?

Certainly, burnout is aptly named. It conjures a number of symbolic images that seem to fit its definition – whether that be running out of fuel or losing your spark. It might also call to mind the idea of burning the candle at both ends, an idiom suggestive of the energy we use up when working long hours (i.e. burning the candle in order to work both early and late). Still, burnout is more than just an abstract concept – and there are a number of formal definitions that can help strengthen our understanding of it.

Burnout is recognized by the World Health Organization (WHO) as an 'occupational phenomenon' and is defined in the following terms:

BURNOUT ACCORDING TO THE WORLD HEALTH ORGANIZATION

Burn-out is a syndrome conceptualized as resulting from chronic workplace stress that has not been successfully managed. It is characterized by three dimensions:

- Feelings of energy depletion or exhaustion.
- Increased mental distance from one's job, or feelings of negativism or cynicism related to one's job.
- Reduced professional efficacy.

Burn-out refers specifically to phenomena in the occupational context and should not be applied to describe experiences in other areas of life.

World Health Organization, 2019

The definition and parameters set by WHO certainly help us to hone and better recognize the signs of burnout when they occur – not merely as a general sensation of stress or overwhelm, but as a real condition that is both work-specific and requiring of serious attention. I also think it's noteworthy that the WHO recognize that burnout is the direct result of workplace stress that 'has not been success-fully managed' – as this clearly indicates that we also have the ability to avoid burnout, if only we can better learn to handle and ultimately eliminate stress.

While the WHO certainly give us a good starting point in terms of formally understanding burnout, I also like the definition provided by Paula Davis in her piece on burnout published in *Forbes*. She writes: 'Burnout is a workplace issue – a chronic process of exhaustion, cynicism, and inef-ficacy caused by a disconnect or an imbalance between key job demands, job resources, and your ability to recover both at work and outside of work' (Davis, 2019).

What I think comes through in both these definitions is the way in which imbalance plays a key role on the slippery slope to overwhelm, stress and – ultimately – burnout itself. It's interesting, too, that Davis mentions the role of 'cynicism' in the development of burnout, as this is an aspect of work dissatisfaction and stress which is less talked about. While we can (and certainly should) recog-nize the ways in which demanding working conditions sap our ability to function well, it's also noteworthy that this is equally bad for morale. When individuals are not only stressed but unhappy, the chances of them achieving good work are decreased.

Understanding these definitions can help us to bring more awareness into our daily working processes so that we might better avoid burnout. That awareness is crucial, too, given how common burnout has become in the modern workplace. Indeed, instead of allowing handy tools to free up mental space so that we might foster cognitive resilience, it seems poor working boundaries have only increased, while the demand to be always on has intensified.

While many people have experienced this phenomenon personally in their working life – regardless of sector or seniority – it is also reflected in recent research. Check out the below findings of a study conducted by the TUC on experiences of increasingly demanding work conditions.

THE WORSENING STATE OF BURNOUT AT WORK – POLLING BY THE TUC FOUND

- 55 per cent of workers reported that work had become intense and demanding.

- 61 per cent of workers reported feeling exhausted at the end of the working day.

- 40 per cent reported they were required to do more work in the same amount of time.

- One in three workers said they were spending more time outside of their contractual hours doing core work activities.

- More than a third of those surveyed also said they were spending more time out of working hours reading, sending and replying to emails than they had the year before.

According to the TUC paper, a number of things had led to these findings – with the increased use of technology, unreasonably high productivity targets, staff shortages, excessive workloads and surveillance all cited as contributing factors to the overall picture of poor working conditions across the board (Prane, 2023).

Of course, this situation is disheartening for a number of reasons – these conditions have led to poorer mental health for workers of all kinds, and, for many more, a sense of disconnect and discontent in their work. What's worse is that this working culture does nothing for true productivity – in fact it is the kiss of death for meaningful work that results in real successes. This is why we must be ever more wary as we enter a new working era with technology much more powerful than anything that has come before.

The robots are coming

It wasn't so long ago that the rise of powerful Artificial Intelligence (AI) seemed like something reserved solely for sci-fi movies. Of course, anyone more tuned into the world of tech will know that many of the tools we use every day are already powered by AI functionality – whether that be the face ID we use to unlock our phones, or the algorithms that power social media, and much more in between!

Still, it's undeniable that AI has reached new, dizzying heights in recent years. Indeed, as it continues to grow in scope and ubiquity, the anxiety that surrounds AI grows also. It's perhaps not a coincidence that we're fearful of AI given all those aforementioned sci-fi narratives – after all, how many films depict kindly, sweet AI androids who just want to look out for humanity? But it hopefully goes without saying that we should not allow such pantomime fears to colour our understanding of AI – especially as it continues to become more integrated with our current work processes.

While there's no doubt that AI is the most disruptive force in the workplace – and arguably the world more broadly – it is only in embracing its potential, and also its nuance, that we can avoid repeating the mistakes of the past. We are already suffering the consequences of allowing our current tech tools to become thoughtlessly mixed in with our modern way of working, but there is just enough time to think seriously about how we might stay abreast and even optimize our work as AI continues to sweep and scale in the world of work.

All this isn't to deny that there are genuine reasons to be concerned about the pace at which AI is changing the working world. Perhaps the biggest and most common fear is job loss. Certainly, this fear isn't without precedent – a report by Goldman Sachs suggests that a huge 300 million full time jobs could be replaced by AI (Vallance, 2023). And let's make no mistake, the future we are already hurtling towards is one in which AI can go toe-to-toe with – and even surpass – humans in many key areas.

Naturally, the working world will change, but that doesn't have to be for ill. Instead, it will mean that many jobs are adjusted or restructured rather than eradicated entirely. There will be an inevitable shift in many roles to spotlight the uniquely human skills that AI cannot so easily replicate. As the report from Goldman Sachs points out,

60 per cent of workers today are in occupations that did not exist in 1940 (Vallance, 2023). It may be hard for us to imagine today the full transformative power of AI and all the ways it will change our perception of what a job is, and how that might align with our broader purpose in life.

The more pressing question, however, is about AI and what it means for focus and burnout at work going forward. There is no easy way to summarize all that AI will do in the coming decades, but in essence it provides an opportunity for us to automate the rote and mundane jobs that are time-intensive but not necessarily complex or creative. But this isn't the only benefit it provides, as it may also fuel actual creative thinking and human ingenuity by better organizing our ideas – and providing us with more inspiration to boot. Some studies have even shown that AI tools lead to productivity spikes and increased job satisfaction – going to show that our mindset surrounding AI may just be the most important way of using it to our broader advantage (Noy et al, 2023).

Discoveries from the 2023 Work Trends Report by Microsoft resonate with this enthusiasm, indicating that AI tools have the potential to alleviate demanding workloads and support employees in coping with burnout (Microsoft, 2023) This sentiment is widely shared amongst workers, as evidenced by a survey conducted by UiPath, an enterprise automation software company. Of the over 6,000 global respondents, 58 per cent expressed the belief that automation can effectively tackle burnout and enhance job satisfaction (UiPath Investor Relations, 2023).

But there's still a catch. Just as the many tools we have today were initially introduced as solutions to streamline productivity and communication, we could once again fall into the trap of allowing the time freed up by AI to be thoughtlessly repurposed into continued BFS. This is the real toxicity of BFS, because it is a state that prioritizes a general sense of 'doing' over actual output. It is also a cultural issue, with colleagues and peers exacerbating the problem by either putting pressure on others to dedicate the same empty time that they do to meaningless work, or even souring working relationships through resentment due to a perceived disparity in commitment to team tasks and projects.

This is exactly why eradicating BFS today is so pressing if we want to achieve our best in the world of tomorrow.

As we will discuss at greater length in coming chapters, it is the exact skills fostered by focused daydream that will be so crucial to succeeding in a new AI-centric world. After all, there is no way to productively hack your way to being more efficient than a machine, and the extent of AI's abilities will only continue to grow in coming years. Do not underestimate, however, the sheer power and complexity of the human brain. As a species, we are naturally engineered for connection making, pattern spotting and novel ideas – but in order to truly lean into these abilities, we need to reallocate our energy supplies so they can better fuel our creative engines.

Summary: a healthier relationship with technology for better productivity

As we journey through this transformative age, we've learned that technology and the growth of the internet, while beneficial in many aspects, have also created a cloud of constant connection and information overload. This growing complexity of life in our digital age has not only changed the speed and general context of our daily lives but also affected the neurological fabric of our brains. No wonder maintaining focus is such a widespread issue, one which is only amplified by the prevalence of stress and burnout.

Look back at our pre-internet, pre-smartphone era – we can clearly see a slower pace of life where intention and dedication were required to, for example, stay in touch with a friend. As we've progressed toward a substantially more convenient and interconnected world, our mental space has been encroached upon and such intentional communication has been rendered rare.

The thoughtless adoption of ever-emerging technological tools and their integration into our work processes undoubtedly contributes to the increasing stress levels and burnout rates, affecting both our personal well-being and professional output.

This technology boom has unavoidably added complexity to our workflow. Instead of simplifying our lives, these 'solutions' have ironically led to a scattered, disorientating mess affecting our cognitive efficiency. Contributing to this scenario is the rise of 'technostress', a condition where our inability to healthily adapt to new technological changes causes chronic mental fatigue.

The problem doesn't end here, though. This constant state of overwhelming technological pressure, coupled with the imbalance between our job demands and available resources, can eventually lead to burnout. Recognized as an 'occupational phenomenon' by the World Health Organization (WHO), burnout is defined as a syndrome due to chronic, unmanaged workplace stress, characterized by exhaustion, cynicism and a reduced sense of efficacy.

Further increasing this concern is the unstoppable growth of AI, giving rise to fears of job losses, changes in job roles, significant shifts in workplace culture and potential complications due to AI integration in long-standing job roles. However, on the flip side, AI also offers opportunities for automating mundane tasks and fostering creative thinking by allowing us to organize our ideas better. It also allows us to focus on the tasks that really matter, improving our general sense of purpose at work.

While AI advancing at an unprecedented rate surely heralds a significant turning point in our work culture, we would do well not to be afraid of it. Remember, falling back into the trap of allowing any time freed up by technology to perpetuate the state of 'doing' we already see in BFS is beneficial to no one. Ultimately, our mindset towards AI will significantly impact its purposeful usage and whether it is really seen as a force for good by most.

As we adapt ourselves to this brave new world of AI, it's critical that we learn to eliminate unfavourable practices such as BFS, and restore the lost equilibrium in our modern working culture.

CHAPTER THREE

Unlock your untapped creative potential

Focused daydreaming – the dreamscape of discovery

Inspiration can be tricky to find, and even trickier to hold on to. All of us have had those flashes of brilliance, when a solution to a complex problem or brilliant idea pops into our head seemingly out of nowhere. Of course, as discussed, such moments are not as spontaneous as they seem, but instead the result of a complex whirring of neurological cogs operating in the background, generally outside our own awareness.

By now, you're hopefully feeling more privy to the power of focused daydreaming. Harnessed correctly, this technique has the power to make us more creative, innovative and resourceful to boot. That's not to mention, of course, the restorative benefits of offering your focused mind some mental respite from the onslaught of demands and tasks most of us experience on a daily basis.

At its core, what focused daydreaming really offers is a chance to unlock the untapped creative potential we all carry inside of us (whether we're aware of it or not). That's why turning focused daydreaming into a daily practice can transform regular breaks into regular breakthroughs via the optimization of your overall cognition.

At this point you may be wondering – if daydreaming is so great, why haven't I heard more about it? While it's certainly the case that most of us have moved through life with little thought for how our own wandering mind might actually facilitate novel ideas, that has not necessarily been the case for some of the world's greatest thinkers.

Indeed, many of the most iconic discoveries, inventions and eureka moments to have graced the pages of history have their roots in daydreaming sessions of one form or another. The very term 'eureka' comes from an Ancient Greek word meaning: 'I have found it!' – a phrase famously uttered by the Greek scholar Archimedes after he stumbled upon a mathematical breakthrough whilst stepping into a bathtub (Ross, 2017). Certainly, Archimedes wasn't the last person to have a great idea whilst in the bath!

Today, we can dive into the nitty-gritty of scientific and psychological research which proves in earnest the power of mind wandering as a vital cognitive act, but that doesn't mean its benefits hadn't been noted anecdotally prior to such discoveries. Even without access to the wealth of neuroscience available today, many of the historic figures we now consider 'creative geniuses' were able to spot – and make use of – the relationship between daydreaming and a state of enhanced mental clarity.

Really, the proof is in the pudding. You don't have to look far to find a wealth of stories that exemplify just how powerful daydreaming can be in sourcing the best ideas that so often subsist just below the surface of our conscious mind – sometimes detectable, but often frustratingly out of reach. While no one is suggesting that daydreaming is the only ingredient in genius insights, there's no denying that in many of the examples we'll go on to discuss, mind wandering enabled such geniuses to reach their best ideas with greater speed, clarity and insight.

Inspiration comes in many forms, and as we'll cover in greater detail later on, one of the key pillars of the focused daydreaming process involves taking time to fuel the creative imagination with material that may ultimately spark new ideas in the subconscious mind. This is exactly why a deep dive into the stories below offers not only good evidence of the power of daydreaming, but fodder for some creative thinking of your own!

So, without further ado, allow me to introduce you to some of the daydreaming greats. From the techniques they used to enhance their daydreaming state to the ideas they uncovered whilst mentally meandering, here are just a few examples of the ways daydreaming has paved the way for innovative thinking and serious creative achievements.

A rocket to Mars

How far-fetched each new advancement seems until it is reached. The technology we today take for granted would have been considered magical just a few centuries ago. While humanity is continually inventing, we also seem to be continually blind to the potential for more developments until we are definitively proven wrong by the emergence of the next big thing. In many ways, this is a tale as old as time – from Galileo to the Wright brothers, many trailblazers were, in their day, faced with the doubt and scepticism of naysayers.

Space travel is perhaps one of the best examples of an incredible feat which not so long ago would have seemed entirely ludicrous. As iconic and bold as President John F Kennedy's famed 1962 'We choose to go to the moon' address may have been, there was a lot of science and theoretical research that preceded even this moment of daring optimism. And so, allow me to introduce you to Robert H Goddard.

It is very possible you have never heard of Goddard, even if you're undoubtedly familiar with the achievements he ultimately set in motion. Often cited as one of the founding fathers of modern rocketry, Goddard is credited with building the world's first liquid-fuelled rocket. The engineering and theoretical work Goddard undertook in his lifetime ultimately paved the way for space travel and exploration, including – of course – the enormous feat of putting man on the moon (Kernan, 1982).

In this way, Goddard's work was the first domino to set in motion the chain of events that ultimately led to modern space exploration. And yet, what preceded all of this? That's right – a seemingly innocuous daydream.

The date was 19th October 1899, and a 17-year-old Goddard had climbed a cherry tree with the intent of pruning its dead branches. Instead, while amidst the foliage, he found that his mind began to wander. Literally presented with a new perspective of the world high above the ground, his thoughts began to turn. This profound moment is something Goddard would later describe in his own words:

> On this day I climbed a tall cherry tree at the back of the barn... and as I looked toward the fields at the east, I imagined how wonderful it would be to make some device which had even the possibility of ascending to Mars, and how it would look on a small scale, if sent up from the meadow at my feet [...] I was a different boy when I descended the tree from when I ascended. Existence at last seemed very purposive. (Stern, 2016)

And so, a seemingly unimportant day and spontaneous daydream inspired the man who would go on to do so much for the future of space travel, and indeed the scale of human achievement more generally. The significance of this daydream was recognized by Goddard himself, who celebrated the date every year, calling it his 'anniversary day', an occasion he marked for the rest of his life. It's certainly harder to characterize daydreams as flippant or frivolous when you put in context what Goddard ultimately went on to achieve as a result of a bit of idle imagining.

It is not coincidental, of course, that Goddard's inspiration came to him while doing something that might ostensibly seem boring or chore-like. It is in moments like these that our imagination is really left free to wander, something which in turn allows our default and executive networks to light up, thus facilitating new connections that are neurologically impossible when we're engaged solely in focused work.

I hear often from people that they simply don't have the time to daydream, but when you consider the creative potential you could be missing out on, I think the more pressing question is, can you really afford not to? By making more quiet space for even seemingly mundane tasks, we leave ourselves open to the potential for a powerful idea or insight which might otherwise have lain dormant in the mind.

The tortured artist fallacy

Few figures are as clouded in myth and mysticism as the archetypal artist. By artist, I of course mean any person who expresses their creativity as an artform – whether that be through music, literature, film, theatre, dance or something else altogether. You'll likely be as familiar as the next person with stereotypes of the so-called 'tortured' artist.

Culturally, we enjoy stories about such figures and seem to relish the idea that creativity is some magical quality randomly bestowed on just a select, talented few. This line of thinking in many ways acts as a scapegoat for our own efforts – because why should we attempt to strive for creativity, when it is something you are either capable of or not?

This, of course, may not seem immediately linked to the topic of finding focus and success at work, but it is actually part of our wider understanding of how brains function – and the ways in which we can mentally attune them to be more creative and resilient in work and life more generally.

The tortured artist stereotype is damaging because it creates a false binary. It is part of the reason I so often hear from others that innovative thinking is simply not 'their thing'. Or – even worse – that creativity is something fluffy and unimportant to real, serious businesspeople. It's easy for us to dismiss the essential role creativity plays in day-to-day life when we attach it to a caricature image of someone 'artsy' or preternaturally talented. Yet the truth is, artist or no, we could all do with more ideas, insight and innovation in our work – especially when we're looking to increase our impact and overall success.

Lest we forget, creativity is something that is inherent in all of us – what really matters is our ability to access it, and indeed to believe in it at all. Treating creativity as something elusive or silly actually limits our own ability to tap into it. Mindset counts for so much in every area of our lives. All of this is to say that while we certainly can't talk about the daydreaming greats without acknowledging some of the many artists who have also used this technique to access elevated levels of artistic insight, we must resist the temptation to dismiss such examples as irrelevant to our own propensity for enhanced creative precision and focus.

It perhaps goes without saying that countless artists – if not almost all of them – have had a tendency to daydream at some point or other. In many ways, it's the chicken and the egg problem: do artists daydream because they're artists, or are they artists because they daydream? Whatever the case, there is undoubtedly an extensive roster of greats who have nourished their own artistic talent with a propensity for mind wandering. And what better example to consider first than that of the Brontë sisters?

Whether you're a fan of a good novel or not, I think we can all recognize the strength of creative imagination that is required to spin a tale about a fictional world. Born in the early 1800s, Emily, Charlotte and Anne Brontë are credited with some of the greatest works of English literature – with novels *Wuthering Heights* and *Jane Eyre* among their titles – but what not so many people know is that they were, first and foremost, great daydreamers.

In fact, there is good reason to suppose a direct line can be drawn between the imaginative play the three sisters undertook with their brother as children, and the novels they penned later in life. A key part of the Brontës' daily routine included long ambling walks (another activity apt to provide daydream fodder) and extensive games of make-believe. These fantastical daydreaming sessions gave the siblings a chance to escape the mundanity of their surroundings, but they also took the act of imagining very seriously – an attitude we could all do with adopting more frequently today.

In 1828, their brother, Branwell, actually began to write down their fabricated adventures and the sisters would soon follow his lead, writing down their own accounts of their many imaginings and stories. As this mental play evolved, what started as little more than a game, became an ongoing writing exercise that paved the way for the great novels that still make up a part of the traditional literary canon today (History Extra, 2020).

The importance of mind wandering, mental play and even plain old idle time is something you'll see again and again when studying the processes of a number of famed artists. Take Edward Hopper, one of the most prevalent artists and realist painters of the 20th century. A telling anecdote from his wife Josephine Nivison Hopper really speaks volumes about how foundational daydreaming is to the creative process. When asked by a journalist what was most challenging about being married to a great artist, Josephine replied, 'It took me a long time to realize that when he is looking out the window, he is working' (Thea, 2018).

Whether it's stories of Agatha Christie plotting her novels whilst doing the dishes, or Henri Matisse's love of staring out of windows, so many great artists have utilized the daydreaming technique to elevate their creative process and sharpen their focus in order to ultimately produce their best work (Thompson, 1966; Brandes, 2020).

But why should we let artists have all the fun? Focused daydreaming has the power to fuel our imagination in exciting ways, regardless of our job role or vocation. Ultimately, how we choose to apply this creative ammunition is up to us, but to ignore its potential altogether seems at best wasteful and at worst foolish.

Inventors and innovators

Eureka! Aha! Ding ding ding! That's right, we're talking about revelation. You know the kind. In a cartoon, such moments are depicted as a lightbulb above the head or lightning striking in the form of a brilliant idea.

In fact, the association between ideas and lightbulbs might be at least partially linked to Thomas Edison – another great thinker who used his dreaming mind to reach new innovative insights. Rather than trying to force out ideas at his desk, Edison would reportedly take a nap holding ball bearings in each hand – as he nodded off, he would lose his grip on the balls, and ultimately drop them. Jolted awake, he could then quickly take note of any ideas that struck him while still connected to the creative pastures of the dreaming mind. One of these 'bright' ideas – if you'll excuse the pun – would eventually lead to the invention of the lightbulb itself, the very thing that is now so synonymous with the iconography of a good idea (Stetka, 2021)!

Given this background, it is hardly surprising that the figure of the inventor is the one we most closely associate with that proverbial 'pop!' of revelation. Today, of course, we might expand the term 'inventor' to encompass any number of other people and roles – whether that be entrepreneurs, scientists or anyone more generally using innovation to change the world with new, creative ideas.

In this sense, we might all think of ourselves as inventors of a kind, even while undertaking daily work. Bizarre as it may sound, anytime we're creative, we are – by definition – creating. In this sense, we are inventing new ways of thinking, and thus bringing something new and original into the world where there wasn't something before.

If you stop a person on the street and ask them to name the first genius to spring to mind, you'll of course get many answers, but one name will inevitably come up time and time again. That name is, of course, Albert Einstein. You don't need me to tell you who Einstein is, or how his work has both laid the foundation for and continued to shape modern physics. His cultural impact is immeasurable, and beyond even his scientific contribution, his general wisdom holds invaluable insight for so many.

What you may not know, however, is how integral daydreaming was to Einstein's overall process. The act of mind wandering – or what he called his 'thought experiments' – was key in helping him uncover some of his most important breakthroughs. In fact, Einstein's theory of relativity supposedly hit him after he spent time imagining the path a light beam might take while moving through space and the universe. It is incredibly telling that one of the most famed and respected thinkers to have walked the earth naturally gravitated towards, and made use of, the daydreaming technique to help nurture his best ideas (Hossenfelder, 2015).

> *Creative scientists are the ones with access to their dreams.* ALBERT EINSTEIN

Now, it goes without saying that we can't all be Einstein. But there's certainly no reason why we shouldn't put to use one of his most universally applicable methods – who knows what it might help us uncover in our own lives? Indeed, that universality is one of the most notable aspects of the mind-wandering technique – Edison and Einstein were hardly the first or last to find revelation whilst lost in the ebb and flow of a mind-wandering session.

Austrian composer Wolfgang Mozart would dream up new music while on long countryside walks, allowing the sounds of nature to weave organically into his compositional ideas, and Sir Issac Newton famously began to contemplate what ultimately became his law of gravity after observing apples falling from a tree (sadly, we may never know whether one of these apples ever did really hit him on the head) (Fries, 2009; Nix, 2018). Others who have stumbled across 'key revelations' while daydreaming include physicist Leo Szilard, organic chemist August Kekulé and biochemist Kary Mullis – and that's to name but a few (Wickelgren, 2011). There's no denying it – the connection between daydreaming and revelation crops up again and again throughout the pages of history. Feats of creativity, it seems, are so often coupled with a mind that has recently wandered astray.

Of course, many of the aforementioned innovators would not have had an awareness of exactly why – in terms of neuroscience – their daydreams resulted in such good ideas, but that doesn't mean they couldn't observe the effect anecdotally. This is perhaps best articulated in a quote attributed to Mozart. Speaking on the connection between good ideas and idle time, he notes: 'When I am travelling in a carriage, or walking after a good meal, or during the night when I cannot sleep; it is on such occasions that ideas flow best and most abundantly'.

Now, with neuroscience to fortify our understanding of how generalized mind wandering can be honed and applied intentionally, we can harness this technique to harvest ideas regularly and efficiently – ball bearings not required!

Dream big and small

There can sometimes be a thin line between inspiration and intimidation. But do not be daunted by the lofty achievements of the aforementioned daydreaming greats. One of my favourite things about the focused daydreaming technique is that it yields unique and personal results for each of us. You don't need to be a great artist, scientist or philosopher to find benefit in it.

Indeed, as this is a tool that explores your own subconscious mind, it will bring forth ideas and insights that are pertinent to you specifically. We will discuss in further detail later how exactly the focused daydreaming tool can be used to help you focus your creative mind in the areas where you'd most like to achieve clarity and insight. Still, I think it's worth noting, too, that creativity isn't the only benefit these great thinkers took from their mind wandering.

Just as rest days are required to build muscle, the benefits of the mental respite offered by regular daydreaming keep the mind sharp and focused. That is why I am such a champion of making this technique a habit, rather than an occasional event, as it not only throws up creative revelations, but the focus and mental resilience required to see those ideas through to their fullest fruition.

In other words, we should not forget that daydreaming is a natural and organic process. We do it every day, sometimes slipping into a different world without even noticing. If we rob ourselves of our daydreams by overworking ourselves and not giving ourselves time, then we're robbing ourselves of a natural process that our brains actually need in order to function healthily.

Activity doesn't always equal progress

It's a common misconception that progress demands our constant, active engagement. Yet consider the parable of the archer: if the archer were to hold the bow perpetually drawn, aiming without release, they would eventually falter, and the arrow's flight would lack strength and precision. Similarly, the mind, if incessantly strained for productivity, ultimately will yield diminishing returns.

It's in this soft space of relaxation – this tender boundary between effort and ease – that the mind synthesizes the fragmented input of our lives into coherent and novel conceptions. When we daydream, our minds are not idly wandering without direction; they are conducting an internal ballet, orchestrating memories, knowledge and emotions into symphonies of innovation.

An often-overlooked aspect of this mental meandering is its effect on our emotional wellbeing. A daydream can transport us to a much-needed vacation, evoke memories of joyous events, or even provide the mental space to empathize with and understand others better. More than a mere mechanism for creativity, it is a wellspring for empathy, compassion and introspection.

A study by the American Psychological Association reveals that focused daydreaming can enhance our capacity for self-awareness and emotional intelligence (Zedelius et al, 2020). By engaging in structured daydreaming, individuals reported increased levels of empathy towards others, better understanding of their own emotional spectrum, and a strengthening of their relationships, both personal and professional.

Reflecting on the extraordinary power harnessed by the great minds of the past, it may become evident that the reprieve facilitated by daydreaming was instrumental not only in their creative process, but also in their emotional fortitude. The capacity to endure hardships, rise above failure and navigate the turbulent waters of criticism is often forged in the quiet moments of mental wandering.

As we acquaint ourselves with the practice of focused daydreaming, we should come to appreciate it as dual-natured: a tool for the cultivation of groundbreaking ideas and a crucible for nurturing emotional depth. In the current age, where mental health is finally gaining the consideration it deserves, the simple practice of allowing oneself to daydream emerges almost as a radical act of self-care.

To daydream is to permit oneself the luxury of unstructured exploration of the mind. It is to acknowledge that despite the wonders of external technology, our most potent instrument of creation exists within the folds of our own brain, awaiting our attention. It is both the genesis of our grandest plans and the playground of our inner child.

In cultivating daydreams, we gain access to a resource simultaneously profound and whimsical. We can embark on epic journeys without leaving the comfort of our room or devise solutions to the most vexing of problems while not moving a muscle physically.

Summary: oxygen needed for your ideas to ignite

In this chapter we have delved into the oft-uncredited yet profound influence of daydreaming on human innovation and creativity. And how this mind wandering has informed many eureka moments, often viewed as sudden and mysterious gifts, and the deeper truth not always seen: that flashes of genius are the fruit of subconscious cognitive processes. On inspection, it's abundantly clear that daydreaming has the power to galvanize our creative energies, offering not just a sanctuary for the harassed mind but also a launchpad for our most imaginative breakthroughs.

Beneath the humdrum of daily life, our mind's capacity for wandering – far from aimlessness – turns out to be a rich tapestry, interweaving creative threads into vibrant mosaics of innovation. Leading thinkers and innovators from history weren't strangers to this phenomenon. From Archimedes in his proverbial bath to the young Robert H. Goddard in his cherry tree, the seeds of spectacular advancement have often been sown in the quiet moments of reverie. Goddard's space exploration dreams underscore the significant potential tucked away in casual daydreams, waiting to bear fruit (pun intended!).

These instances challenge the conventionally touted paradigm that creativity hinges on a mysterious essence bestowed upon only a chosen few. Exploring examples of great thinkers of the past it becomes clear that daydreaming transcends any one occupation or type of person. It is not the exclusive domain of artists, inventors or geniuses, but a universal currency of the mind that has the potential to enrich every aspect of our work and personal lives.

Not to be overlooked is the insight into the mental and emotional implications of daydreaming. Beyond creative leaps, these moments of mental wandering act as a balm for the soul, a conduit for empathy and a foundation for enhancing one's emotional intelligence. We must recognize the power within our minds and embrace this form of self-care with intention.

Imagine a future where focused daydreaming forms a harmonious counterbalance to the rigour of your daily routines, offering not just respite but also the oxygen for your most profound ideas to ignite.

CHAPTER FOUR

The misinterpreted mental voyage

'Daydreaming may sound like a mental luxury but its purpose is deadly serious.'
DOUGLAS FOX, 'THE SECRET LIFE OF THE BRAIN', *NEW SCIENTIST*

If I ask you to picture someone daydreaming, what do you see? Perhaps you imagine a person staring absentmindedly out of a window, or somebody with a glazed-over expression, zoned out in the middle of a conversation. You might also focus on the idea of the daydream itself – a cloud above the head filled with the swirling colours of the daydreamer's imagination. Naturally, each person visualizes daydreaming differently, reflecting the diverse and intricate nature of the daydreams we individually experience and become immersed in.

In this sense, daydreaming is a slippery concept. While we certainly have some shared understanding of what it is, individual perceptions differ (in fact, going back to what you imagined just a moment ago can likely tell you a lot about your own perceptions – did you imagine the daydreamer as young or old, for example?). Hopefully, by now, you are already sensing your perspective on daydreaming starting to shift, but out in the real world, the most common attitude encountered regarding daydreaming is one of apathy and indifference.

Naturally, this speaks to all the ways daydreaming is misunderstood and underestimated in daily life. This is likely a byproduct of historic attitudes towards daydreaming, which is why we must be careful not to allow residual negativity to colour our perspective today. That's because the subtle and implicit ways we perceive a subject naturally affect how we then approach it in real life. In other words, if you're carrying around misconceptions about the power of daydreaming, you're much less likely to engage with it in a serious and meaningful way going forward.

Even if you feel your views of daydreaming are broadly neutral, or even positive, there is still great merit in getting to grips with the mechanics of the most persistent daydreaming myths. After all, being hit with a list of facts isn't the only way to understand a subject. By dissecting the fallacies that taint our understanding of mind wandering, we can begin to appreciate more fully the scope and potential of this activity as a real, neurological tool that can be applied to our advantage.

You are more than likely familiar with old sayings that denigrate daydreaming – 'an idle mind is the devil's playground' is one idiom that comes to mind – but it's important to understand the cultural workings that underpin such maxims. After all, it's not surprising that in the past daydreaming was viewed negatively. In bygone eras, work was much more clearly bookmarked within the day. In these periods, daydreaming during allotted work hours might have been considered undesirable, but other opportunities for daydreaming would have been frequent and naturally occurring outside these hours – and in ways we no longer experience in the modern world.

Today, we have constant and abundant access to others, as well as limitless forms of entertainment at our fingertips. As previously discussed, quiet moments are now few and far between – while work frequently bleeds into all other areas of our life via the omnipresence of our devices. Of course, our attitude towards work has evolved in this time, too. We now have a greater awareness of the importance of the need for work-life balance in general, and how key it is that we prioritize our own wellbeing. Yet, all too frequently, we fail to put this well-intentioned theory into practice.

In many ways, we might think about the role of daydreaming in daily life as akin to the role of physical activity. The idea of a gym would have seemed totally bizarre just a few generations ago, but today we recognize that a gym and exercise routine can offer us an easier way of fitting physical health around our busy schedules. Similarly, where once mind wandering was an organic part of many people's days, today we really need to bring more structure and intention into the process in order to retain the benefits it naturally provides, and also to enhance its effects in our daily work.

That is why we will go specifically and methodically through some of the most common daydreaming myths, explore how they came to be, and examine more closely why we shouldn't be swayed by these incorrect perceptions. From its depiction as something childish or time wasting through to the forms of daydreaming that can genuinely have negative effects – it's time to burst the bubble on daydream myths for good!

Daydreaming is for children

The connection between childhood and daydreaming is a longstanding one. Many of us will associate daydreaming with stories such as the fantastical *Alice in Wonderland*, or remember it as something we'd be chastised for when our attention wandered during school hours. Most of us take for granted, too, that children are more creative than adults. The evidence for this is plentiful; with vivid imaginations and a propensity for fun and games, children seem to possess naturally more adventurous imaginations than we do as grown-ups.

Yet, this is more than just anecdotal knowledge. A landmark study in 1969, which utilized a test used by NASA to help them find highly creative engineers, went some distance in proving that children are genuinely more creative than adults – and that this trait, which is seemingly innate in us, wanes over time. The study found that of 1,600 children tested at age five, 98 per cent scored in the highly creative range. But then, tested again five years later, just 30 per cent of the same sample group still ranked as highly creative. By the time the children were 15, only 12 per cent were still classed in this top category. Furthermore, the same test given to 250,000 adults over the age of 25 revealed that a meagre 2 per cent scored as highly creative (Land and Jarman, 1992).

As George Land, the conductor of this study, writes: 'What we have concluded is that non-creative behaviour is learned.' In other words, creativity is not some elusive trait or talent, but something almost all of us innately have, but ultimately lose through the process of assimilation into society.

Really, this is hardly surprising. When we talk about thinking outside the box, we rarely stop to question what the box is. In many ways, 'box' is a fitting metaphor, as what this really refers to is the frameworks and mindset we learn to subscribe to as we are moulded by the education system, work and other people. This scaffolding provides our framework for seeing the world, and literally boxes us in, making us less likely to perceive certain possibilities or engage in more lateral modes of thinking.

All this is to say, daydreaming may indeed be associated with children, but it might also just be one of the many reasons that kids are more creative than us adults to begin with. And is a propensity for creativity really something we'd like to avoid? While it's true that the term 'childish' is generally thought of as an insult, I would argue that we could all achieve some great things by becoming more child-like in our day-to-day lives.

Children are sponges. They hunger for knowledge and are propelled by curiosity. They are also resilient, able to bounce back from setbacks and retain a positive mindset in daunting circumstances. This is arguably part and parcel of the ongoing learning and evolution that occurs during childhood, but it is also a neurological trait. It is already known that children have greater brain plasticity than adults (Johnston et al, 2009). But did you know that this same plasticity can also be enhanced in adults through the act of mind wandering itself?

Take a fascinating study undertaken by researchers at Harvard Medical School. Their research tracked the brain activity of mice as they looked at two separate images with distinct patterns. The researchers found that in moments of respite, the mice's thoughts would naturally drift back to the images they had seen (something they gauged through monitoring the patterns of neurons fired and matching them to the patterns fired when the images were first shown to the mice).

Ultimately, what surprised the researchers was that the slightly altered pattern of neurons fired during mind-wandering moments (when the mice recalled the images) would go on to impact the neurons which then fired when the mice were shown the images a second time. In fact, this process – one the researchers dubbed 'representational drift' – was ongoing, until the neurons that fired in the mice's brains when faced with the images became increasingly distinct.

While this might sound like a lot of impenetrable neuroscience to you and me, to the researchers it suggested that daydreaming plays a key function in neuroplasticity. Their findings indicate that the mind wandering that occurred when the mice's thoughts drifted back to the original images played a role in their ability to learn, and ultimately distinguish one image from another later on. For mice, this trait may have evolutionary benefits in terms of identifying potential predators – but for humans, the researchers concluded, the process is simply 'an efficient way to learn about the world' (Nguyen et al, 2024).

I cannot overstate how invaluable brain plasticity is to us both at work and in our wider lives. It is a neurological trait that allows us to be more creative and resilient so that we are able to learn and adapt in new or challenging environments. When we make more time for daydreaming, we are not being childish, but in fact becoming more child-like. It allows our brains to become more malleable, thus giving our creativity the space to flourish and the focused mind the space it needs to learn and recharge in moments of respite.

While we might agree that daydreaming is something children naturally make more time for – after all, their imaginations tend to be more powerful and frequently in use – to claim it is only for children is reductive. After all, who amongst us couldn't benefit from more creativity, flexibility and resilience? To disdain daydreaming just because of its association with children is to miss out on a whole world of creative potential and other neurological benefits!

Not everyone can daydream

I am always surprised to hear people express worry about their ability to daydream 'properly'. Often this response comes about after we have already begun discussing daydreaming as a potential tool for enhancing creativity and focus. While most people will admit that their thoughts sometimes drift away from the present moment, as soon as they hear about focused mind wandering as a genuine tool for enhanced focus, they suddenly begin to doubt themselves.

Arguably, this is a part of human nature. We can be naturally sceptical of so-called 'quick fixes' – and also insecure about our ability to apply a new skill or tool effectively, especially when it doesn't fit neatly within our current worldview. It's really crucial we address this mis-perception, however, as the instinct to avoid trying some-thing new owing to a fear of failure is ultimately a form of perfectionism.

Ostensibly, striving for perfection might not sound all that bad – but in reality it is often a hindrance to good work, impeding our ability to take action and even damag-ing our self-esteem. Placing daydreaming on a pedestal as some creative ability beyond your power will hamper your ability to engage in it meaningfully. And ultimately, this perception is not accurate, anyway. Daydreaming isn't just something we all do occasionally, but an inherent part of our neurological wiring.

In fact, one study found that our minds are wandering almost half the time we're awake (47 per cent of the time to be exact) – so the question isn't whether you can daydream at all, but whether you are daydreaming in a productive and helpful way (Killingsworth and Gilbert, 2010). I say this because, unfortunately, not all daydreams were created equal.

Of course, as discussed in previous chapters, we might define daydreaming in a number of ways. In some senses, any time our attention is diverted from the current moment we are 'daydreaming' – allowing thoughts of things not currently present to flicker through our mind – but by this definition, worrying and dwelling might also be considered daydreaming. This is something of a dangerous loophole. It is also likely why I am sometimes met with scepticism when advocating for the benefits of daydreaming. People will tell me their thoughts are constantly elsewhere, and yet they don't seem to have any of the associated benefits. But they're missing something crucial!

True daydreaming is characterized by free-flowing thoughts. The type of daydreaming we engage in, as well as the framework that sits around the tool, is incredibly important to the results we ultimately reap. While I will go into further details of the specifics of focused daydreaming later on, I think that idea of a 'wandering' mind is what's really key here. The kind of thinking that sits in one place, or chews over the same thing again and again, should not be thought of in the same way as the type of daydreaming that brings brain benefits.

That is why it's integral that making time for daydreaming doesn't become an excuse to make time for worrying. Of course, we all fall victim to worry sometimes, and that's nothing to be ashamed of. What's crucial is being able to identify such moments for what they are and – where possible – do our best to short-circuit the momentum that causes general worry to spiral into full-blown anxiety. Personally, I tend to think of worrying, dwelling and wallowing as forms of stagnant thinking. While your thoughts might not technically be in the moment, they're also not freewheeling and making connections.

I think it's important to note, too, that daydreaming is a highly subjective experience. Our brains all work differently thanks to the rich neurodiversity present throughout the general population. Never forget, daydreaming is something that comes naturally to each of us – and so long as your thoughts are flowing and broadly positive, there's no way to do it wrong. While it's true that some studies have found a correlation between more fantastical daydreams – as well as daydreams with more personal meaning – and higher levels of creativity, what really matters is that the daydreams feel positive and natural to you (Zedelius et al, 2020).

For example, you might be a more visual person, and therefore your daydreams may prioritize that perspective over other senses. Some people prefer to think in linear terms, while others follow a pattern of thoughts that are all topsy-turvy. Perhaps your natural tendency when daydreaming is to comb back through old happy memories rather than dreaming up theoretical worlds or future scenarios. Daydreaming can be as simple as imagining what to cook for dinner or planning a new outfit. In fact, given the nature of daydreams themselves, a single mind-wandering session might ping you between any number of these seemingly unrelated topics.

That's because the best daydreaming is characterized by connectivity – like frogs jumping between lily pads, one thought tends to lead to another. Undoubtedly, we have all seen or experienced this at one time or another. A person zones out, only to drop back into the conversation with a seemingly random comment or question – the tide of their thoughts taking them far away from the present conversation. While in the moment this might seem amusing, or even frustrating, the reality is the daydreamer's mind has drifted downstream to new creative pastures, and likely gathered a few ideas in the process.

In short, not only can everyone daydream – everyone does. What matters more is how you approach mind wandering, and your ability to distinguish it from more stagnant forms of thinking such as worrying or dwelling. Knowing this offers a positive incentive to really let loose when you feel your thoughts naturally go a-wandering.

We will explore in later chapters some of the best prompts for getting yourself into a positive daydreaming state, and there's certainly plenty of scope to experiment and find out what starting point works best for you. But before that point, it's important we all recognize the vast daydreaming potential we carry inside. With a bit of intention, we can make this natural propensity something genuinely powerful.

Daydreaming is bad for productivity

I'll admit, this particular myth at least has the veneer of truth. After all, how can one be productive whilst daydreaming? The short answer, of course, is that you can't. But taking a step back, the more pertinent question isn't whether daydreaming is a productive activity in itself, but whether it can make you more productive in your life overall. The answer to this question, in my opinion, is an unequivocal yes.

Still, it's not hard to see why daydreaming gets a bad rap. It happens involuntarily, and in moments of boredom we're more likely to lose the thread of our attention and zone out or let our mind wander elsewhere. This is one of many reasons we have such a strong association between daydreaming and procrastination. No wonder, then, that the perception of daydreaming as a wasteful activity is one of the biggest and most pervasive mind-wandering myths.

But let's look at this another way, if boredom triggers our daydream response, then there must be some evolutionary benefit to this state in the first place. Indeed, in moments of tedium, daydreaming can relieve boredom and actually put our brain to better use elsewhere. In fact, in many ways mind wandering can be very helpful in keeping us on task when the work we're faced with isn't mentally demanding. In the time before smartphones, standing in line at the shop or working through the dishes was something made infinitely more enjoyable via the outlet of daydreaming.

Of course, more difficult 'thinking' work cannot be done at the same time as engaging in daydreaming, but spending more time allowing our thoughts to drift in those idle or dull moments when they do occur (whether that be when out on a walk or ploughing through your chores) can actually boost your productivity when the time arrives to be on the ball and on-task.

I sometimes think of this whole concept as a game of whack-a-mole; when you deny your brain the opportunity to run free in the more organic mind-wandering moments, this need will simply pop up elsewhere, and likely at a less convenient time to boot. This is one reason our thoughts so regularly go astray during inopportune work moments – such as during a meeting or while faced with an important task. Our mind, having been denied the natural respite of regular mind wandering, responds to the stress of the situation at hand by simply going offline. This then often leads to frustration, which makes us feel negatively about daydreaming and more likely to avoid it in other situations.

All of this is not to mention the many neurological benefits of mind wandering that naturally improve your focus and refine your creativity so that you might engage with a given task with more tenacity and enthusiasm than you would have if functioning at a suboptimal neuro-level (an issue that is especially pronounced when you are facing burnout or overwhelm). What's more, the very act of making more time for focused daydreaming can, in itself, offer productivity benefits.

The problem with the chronic state of Busy Fool Syndrome (BFS) in the workplace at large is that our very perception of productivity itself is warped. When we're rushing around, hair always on fire, of course the idea of making time for doing nothing sounds at best irresponsible, and at worst downright scary. But unless we want to be like that poor frog slowly being boiled alive, we must learn to hop out of the pot from time to time so that we can cool off and protect ourselves from the adverse effects of stress and burnout. In fact, many people find that by carving out time for themselves to engage in focused daydreaming, they're able to be more proactive in using their remaining time.

After all, this is the crux of the BFS issue. We may feel that we don't have enough time in our day to do all that we need to, but in actual fact we are labouring under the delusion that we're being more productive than we actually are. So much of the workday at present is spent hopping between unimportant forms of communication and wading through to-do's without actually ticking anything off. When we make space in our day to be away from this always-on but rarely productive system, we begin to see more clearly all the unuseful modes of working we're engaged in, and so are able to eliminate them.

A study published in the *Journal of Applied Behavior Analysis* found that the frequency and duration of breaks during the workday may play a pivotal role in an individual's ability to achieve a heightened level of productivity (Nastasi et al, 2023). This research meticulously scrutinized the productivity of 16 undergraduate students under varied conditions. In the first session, half of the participants observed a regimen of five-minute breaks every 20 minutes, whereas the other half did not take any breaks. Subsequently, the roles were reversed in the second session. A control session, where breaks were optional, was also included for comparative analysis.

The study found that a very noteworthy 75 per cent of participants exhibited significantly enhanced productivity during sessions with structured breaks. Interestingly, during a session where breaks were optional, most of the students actually took more breaks than they did when the breaks were more clearly scheduled. What's so fascinating here is the suggestion that, yes, breaks improve our productivity – but also that having intention (i.e. carving out time for breaks ahead of time) can be best at helping us stay focused and on-task, without giving in to temptation to procrastinate or avoid work.

Of course, this study was looking at breaks in a broad sense – when you consider the scope to use this carved-out time specifically for daydreaming, the productivity benefits naturally increase. As already discussed in this chapter, mind wandering is strongly connected to neuroplasticity, a trait which holistically enables us to work better, more flexibly – whether that be in making the most of a new creative opportunity or being able to bounce back when faced with challenges. To put it simply: daydreaming is actually a salve for chronic procrastinators and has incredible scope to boost rather than hinder productivity.

Daydreaming, a gateway to overthinking?

Overthinking. Something we are probably all too familiar with, and who's to say that daydreaming doesn't cause the brain to overthink even more? After all, if we're sitting in our offices or working from home thinking about the future or past, how can we be productive? Aren't we overthinking when we keep daydreaming about scenarios for our future self instead of focusing on our present self? Yet, this is to misunderstand the nature of focused daydreaming. It is not the rusty nail, it is the tool you use to pry out the rusty nail in order to replace it with a shiny brand new one. In other words, focused daydreaming does not always lead to a negative flow of overthinking as some may think.

First, though, let's put into perspective the extent to which people are willing to go in order to avoid their own thoughts. In a study published in 2014, adults were given the option of either entertaining themselves with their own thoughts for 15 minutes or giving themselves minute but painful electric shocks. A shocking 65 per cent of men chose to receive the shocks, along with 25 per cent of women (Wilson et al, 2014). In another experiment conducted in 2022, six experiments were conducted in which participants were asked to sit and wait in a quiet room without doing anything (Hatano et al, 2022).

It was predicted that the participants would enjoy this task and wouldn't have a problem with engaging with their own thoughts, but this was not the case. Instead, researchers say the 'under-appreciation of thinking' meant that participants actively sought out ways to avoid thinking, such as scrolling through their phones on news outlets or social media. Both experiments reveal the lengths people are willing to go to in order to avoid the simple activity of sitting and thinking. It could not be more obvious that we use distraction as a coping technique, and in a world full of tempting distractions like social media we need to force ourselves past these sinkholes for our attention in order to allow ourselves to be comfortable with our own thoughts before we can then begin to daydream.

Of course, as humans with complex emotions, we often fixate on the stresses of our lives, trying to figure out ways in which to resolve them in the hope it will save us from future stress – though naturally it rarely does. We feel that if we can eliminate the problem quickly, then we won't have to think about it anymore. However, sometimes it's not as simple as that. Some problems cannot be solved immediately, yet we still continue to fixate on them, and thus our brain's way of protecting us from future stress only leads to more stress for us in the present, as well as in the future. And, of course, it is not a secret that stress leads to that awful rush of anxiety and – more often than not – a choppy, unhealthy stream of overthinking.

I'm sure you're glad to hear that there is good news, too. The brain is a powerful organ and, although it's hard to cure a tricky case of overthinking, we can learn to have more control over our thoughts with patience, practice and intention.

As we have already discussed, daydreaming is not a 'lazy' pastime, nor is it only a distraction or a way to escape reality. But how do you use it to help slow down the tide of anxious thought?

First, it is imperative that you know how to think for pleasure. A study was conducted in 2017 in which participants were contacted four times a day for a week and asked to rate what they had been thinking about (Westgate and Wilson, 2016). In some cases, participants were provided with a 'thinking aid', in which they were given pleasurable things to think about. The participants who received the 'thinking aid' found the experience to be much easier and more enjoyable, showing just how easy it is for people to engage in pleasurable thoughts when they are given simple prompts. Although thinking can be a cognitively difficult activity in some cases, a simple framework can make the task of thinking for pleasure easier and more enjoyable.

Naturally, we can apply the same logic to daydreaming in order to avoid overthinking. On occasions where we feel more prone to overthinking, we can sit down and create pre-planned things to choose from before we begin daydreaming. This can then help turn it into an enjoyable activity, becoming a tool to help your creativity instead of a nuisance that triggers your brain to overthink.

Myth busting in your own life

It goes without saying that this isn't an exhaustive list of all the myths and misconceptions that inhibit our cultural understanding of daydreaming – but hopefully it does at least go some way in helping you to understand just how erroneous these myths are.

Now, when I ask you to picture someone daydreaming, the image that comes to mind might still be much the same as it was before – but what's changed, I hope, is your association with that image. Far from seeing the daydreamer as someone childish or lazy, you can now connect this mental activity with a broader picture of neurological wellbeing and holistic work–life balance.

Of course, you might also find the attached image has changed. Perhaps you see the daydreamer in a different context now – taking purposeful time out of work rather than bunking off. You might also see an adult where before you saw a child or student. Who knows, maybe you now even imagine this scenario in the first-person perspective, seeing yourself lost in a daydream rather than envisioning someone else!

Whatever the case, the main thing is you take this myth-busting ethos forward with you into the wider world. Whether that means taking a moment to remind yourself that unwanted daydreams are likely a consequence of an overstimulated or burned-out mind, rather than an issue with mind wandering itself. Plus, don't forget to spread the word! We break down misconceptions by calling them out and discussing openly your own experiences with daydreaming, especially the positive ones that may have led you to breakthroughs you might not have reached otherwise.

Daydream myth	Daydream fact
Daydreams confuse us and muddy the cogency of our thoughts.	Free-moving mind wandering is associated with increased alpha wave activity in the brain, a trait that has been linked with better performance on creative tasks (Suttie, 2021).
Responsible and serious adults don't daydream.	According to estimates by experts, we spend as much as 47 per cent of our waking hours daydreaming. In other words, it's something we all do, whether we admit it or not (Sleep Foundation, 2021).

Daydream myth	Daydream fact
Your brain turns off and becomes unproductive when you daydream.	Research from the University of British Columbia found that our brains are more active than previously thought when engaged in mind wandering, and that this process can be linked to heightened problem-solving skills (Science Daily, 2009).
Making time for daydreaming will result in less work completed.	One 2012 study found a notable link between regular daydreaming breaks and not only increased creativity, but increased productive output (Baird et al, 2012).

Summary: the hallmark of a brain in its element

Throughout this chapter we have journeyed across a landscape clouded by misperception and bias, shining a light on the myths that shroud daydreaming in negativity and misunderstanding. Drawing back this veil, we can see daydreaming for what it actually is: a dynamic and engaging mental process that enhances one's creative faculties, sharpens problem-solving skills and promotes a flexible, resilient mind.

At its core, daydreaming defies the age-old stereotypes of idle minds and wasteful indulgence. Instead, it emerges as a ubiquitous and natural cognitive state – one that does not discriminate by age, profession or disposition. Everyone daydreams, from children lost in play to adults navigating the complexities of work and life. It is part of our brain's innate ability to roam, freely and untethered, making serendipitous connections and stumbling upon novel ideas.

Far from being a sign of a distracted or unproductive individual, daydreaming is the hallmark of a brain in its element – engaging with the world in a unique and deeply personal way. It is the mind's playground, where curiosity leads to discovery and where, as we now know, creative solutions to everyday problems are often found.

Daydreaming is not the exclusive realm of children or the sole hallmark of a distracted mind. Instead, it is a ubiquitous experience that wields the ability to evolve our thinking, drive our creativity and enhance our productivity – and in ways far beyond what has conventionally been believed or understood.

Mind wandering isn't a residual artefact of childhood imagination; it is a testament to our brain's capacity for adaptability and innovation. It carries us beyond the confines of rigid thought patterns and linear problem solving, guiding us towards a horizon brimming with possibilities.

The practice of daydreaming empowers us to transcend routine thinking and tap into a wellspring of creativity and resilience.

CHAPTER FIVE

Doing less to achieve more

Let me start by saying: I know how it sounds. Much like claiming you can 'eat more to weigh less' or 'stay awake to sleep more', telling people they can achieve more by doing less is bound to raise a few eyebrows. At least on the surface level, it sounds – to put it bluntly – nonsensical. After all, motivated action is a rather crucial part of getting things done. So, how exactly can you achieve more things by doing less? Hopefully, by the end of this chapter you'll have a much clearer idea of how exactly this can be the case and – even better – insight into how you can do it yourself.

Still, let me begin by assuaging your fears. I promise I am not some snake oil salesman or conman bent on spinning you a tall tale. Instead, what I'm proposing is a crucial and arguably seismic shift to your mindset which will allow you to be more productive, even whilst spending less time at your desk. As we've discussed at length by this point, Busy Fool Syndrome (BFS) has become the insidious and often invisible force driving so many modern workers towards burnout. What's worse, this syndrome has a tendency to sap energy and poison morale, but it does so without offering any tangible productivity benefits to the individuals caught in the thick of its malaise.

It's hardly surprising, then, that the presence of BFS – and the ambition to rise above it – is highly relevant when it comes to being able to achieve more by doing less. In many ways, what we're setting out here is a way to turn BFS on its head. If BFS is all about doing an endless number of things without achieving much at all, what I am presenting is a way to be more strategic in order to achieve more of your goals without withering away at your desk hour after hour.

One of the key issues with BFS is that we seem to have assumed that simply by being 'at work' – whether that's actually in an office, or simply online working remotely – we are inherently embodying a form of productivity. Sadly, this is not the case. In fact, this can be a dangerous fallacy that leads to a competitive culture in which people equate hours worked directly with overall productivity levels. It is for this reason we so often see toxic work environments crop up, with employees who stay late feeling resentful of those who leave on time.

Now, I'm not at all trying to suggest that working late or over the set hours isn't sometimes a necessity – when we have a big deadline or tricky project, it is occasionally inevitable that an extra push is needed in order to get things over the line. The issue comes when this is a permanent state of being, with individuals evidencing their 'productivity' via how many hours they've worked or how stressed they feel, rather than through the actual work they've produced in the time they've been present. What's worse, this kind of environment frequently leaves team members feeling isolated, and can even lead to adverse mental health consequences for those unable to stay abreast. It is a race-to-the-bottom scenario, and as with all situations of this kind, everyone ultimately loses.

I don't want to underestimate the importance of presenteeism at work. It's hardly a secret that absenteeism is undesirable for productivity, whichever way you slice it. For companies, absenteeism is associated with reduced profit margins – for teams and colleagues, losing a member of staff for a day or two can mean increased pressure and unmanageable workloads (SPARK, 2017). Striving to overcome BFS isn't about creating a working culture in which there is no accountability, but instead about shifting the focus so that we can think about how we work, looking beyond the time we spend working and thinking more about what we're actually getting done – both in terms of output and quality.

If you've read to this point in the book, you won't be surprised to hear that focused daydreaming is a key ingredient in the recipe to achieving this success. In fact, when I say you can achieve more by doing less, I am specifically referring to the act of daydreaming. Mind wandering, of course, is technically a non-task. It's about throwing off the shackles of focus and allowing your thoughts to roam where they may. But, as we will explore, making time for this kind of 'doing nothing' might just enable you to achieve more than you ever thought possible.

Befriend your brain

How is your brain doing? It's not exactly a question you're likely to ponder often, or indeed one you'd ask others. Naturally, we're aware on some level that the state of our brain is directly correlated with our own wellbeing and mood. All of our experiences and emotions are filtered through the brain, after all. It is the conduit through which we experience life – and also the primary tool that enables us to engage and participate in the world around us. While we won't get into philosophical debates about consciousness and selfhood here, I think it's fair to say that the state of our brain, or rather our thinking, has a huge impact on both our overall happiness and our ability to be successful in work.

And yet, despite this fact, the brain is – for most of us – a mystery. While we might have a rough idea of what it looks like, a mass of wrinkly grey-pink stuff in our head, we are not really privy to its inner workings. Inevitably, there are many complex gradients of information that make up the neuroscience field, but even just by understanding the basic functioning of the brain we can begin to learn how to better use it to our advantage. Just as a knowledge of different spices and herbs can improve the way someone cooks, knowing what's going on under the hood can give us context to how we might fix our focus and achieve more.

So, to start, let's get acquainted with the basics of our brain. Needless to say, there is a near-infinite amount of detail we could explore here, but for our purposes here is a brief outline of the key parts of the brain:

- **The frontal cortex.** You can think of this area as the brain's boss. Situated at the front, it handles important tasks like paying attention, making decisions, planning our actions and keeping our social behaviour in check. We call this bundle of responsibilities the 'executive function'.
- **The parietal lobe.** This area deals with touch sensations and coordinates our movements. Think of it as the brain's stage manager for how we feel things and move around.
- **The occipital cortex.** This is where the brain processes what we see. Picture it like layers of a cake, each layer working on a different piece of visual information. This part helps us make sense of the world around us.
- **The temporal lobes.** These two parts are like the language experts of the brain. Situated on the left side of the brain, we've got the Wernicke's and Broca's areas – kind of like our brain's translator and speech coach. Wernicke's area helps us understand speech, while Broca's area helps us speak.

In addition to these areas, we also have the basal ganglia (which manages our actions), the hippocampus (which handles memory) and the amygdala (where we process emotions such as fear). All these parts work in unison as a neurological team, coming together to create the overall masterpiece that is you (Farnsworth, 2020).

But what exactly does overwhelm and burnout do to the brain? In a discussion with *Yale Daily*, leading expert in neuroscience and psychology, Professor Amy Arnsten, shed some light on the impact of uncontrollable stress on the prefrontal cortex (an area that is also the newest part of the brain in evolutionary terms). As pointed out above, this crucial region governs higher cognition, abstract thought and working memory among other executive functions – of course, all these skills are undeniably integral to our ability to achieve good work (Yup, 2022). So, when this part of the brain comes under strain, we necessarily experience other knock-on effects – ones that can ultimately lead to burnout.

Interestingly, Arnsten also emphasizes the pivotal role that perceived control over stressors plays in determining the impact such pressures will actually have on the brain. When individuals feel overwhelmed by tasks they perceive to be beyond their capabilities – even if they actually are capable of tackling them – the stress response kicks in, weakening the prefrontal cortex and reinforcing more primitive parts of the brain.

This reaction, according to Arnsten, might have held survival value at earlier points of human evolution – as she points out, freezing when encountering a dangerous animal such as a bear can actually keep you safe by helping you stay undetected. The issue is, most of what we face in our daily life is very different from the direct and immediate danger our ancestors would have faced (Yup, 2022). This research does at least shed some light on why that frustrating, paralysed feeling is such a common response to overwhelm at work. What's more, it also suggests that by learning to better manage and negate general stress, we can more readily avoid the undesirable cognitive symptoms that come along with it.

One Cornell study highlighted by Arnsten also looked at the impact of psychosocial stress (in this instance, the stress of intensive preparation for a major exam) on the prefrontal cortex. The study used neuroimaging to observe the brains of medical students and found that the stressor of exam preparation weakened the connectivity of the prefrontal network, leading to impaired function and attention regulation (Liston, McEwen and Casey, 2009).

Referencing the study, clinical assistant professor of psychiatry Mark Rego explained that observable break-down symptoms – such as difficulty concentrating and emotional outbursts – are key indicators of impaired prefrontal function. However, the study also revealed that in healthy individuals, the plasticity of the prefrontal cortex allowed for these cognitive impairments to be reversed after a month of reduced stress (Williams, 2021).

This is why Rego proposes the concept of 'frontal fatigue' – a vulnerability in the prefrontal cortex that is exacerbated by repeated cycles of mental breakdown and recovery. Undoubtedly, frontal fatigue is something more and more of us are experiencing in daily working life. This is bad news as it is this exact fatigue which, left unaddressed, leads to burnout and even depression. The toxic loop of BFS can keep us trapped in a working context that chips away at the functioning of our frontal lobe, ultimately leaving us ever more vulnerable to impaired executive operation and burnout.

The good news, however, is that – by contrast – through maintaining a healthy brain and neurological balance we can build resilience in the brain in order to optimize its function and simultaneously protect ourselves from undesirable mental fallout. How? Well, that brings us on to my next point. Spoiler alert: it doesn't involve spending more time at your laptop.

Neurodiversity and focused daydreaming

As we delve deeper into understanding the complexities of the brain and how it functions, it feels important we also take another look at neurodiversity. As we've touched upon earlier on, neurodiversity refers to the rich and varied cognitive differences that exist amongst everyone – while 'neurodivergent', as a term, refers to those with a neurological difference such as autism, ADHD, ADD, dyslexia, dyscalculia and dyspraxia.

For many neurodivergent individuals, daydreaming isn't inherently a distraction or an obstacle; instead, it is a natural, habitual way of thinking, and in many cases primes the brain to be creative and innovative in less obvious ways. People with ADD and ADHD, for instance, often engage in what's known as 'hyper-focus', where they become engrossed in an activity to the exclusion of all else. Anecdotally, it seems that this intense concentration happens most frequently during tasks that stimulate the imagination.

Similarly, individuals with dyslexia frequently exhibit impressive visual thinking skills. While dyslexia may affect an individual's literacy skills, it can at the same time enhance their capacity for big-picture thinking, problem solving and creative pursuits. In other words, the very mechanisms that cause difficulties in one area of the brain may facilitate advanced abilities in another. It's only when we work in a cookie-cutter way, expecting the same things from everyone, that we run into trouble around this.

While many people assume that the creativity associated with neurodivergence is inherent, there's good reason to think this creativity actually arises from the fact that this neurological make-up allows ND individuals to see things from a fresh perspective. This is why focused daydreaming, when put to use, can also make you more creative – providing a regular cognitive reset that helps you see things from new perspectives and with enhanced clarity.

Take a break – no, seriously

I'm here to tell you to take a break. In fact, I'm telling you to take multiple breaks. Every single day. I'm insisting that more breaks will improve your work, and also your focus. For most people, this is welcome advice. We're more commonly used to hearing that good work requires that we push on – that success is directly correlated with dedication to the hustle.

This is because the message we receive by osmosis from the business world, as well as culture at large, is that the exhausting pursuit of our most ambitious goals is the only way to get ahead. And, undeniably, hard work is a valuable asset in any field. But pouring energy into work without strategy is like furiously jogging on the spot and hoping to run a marathon – you'll work your muscles, sure, but you won't be getting anywhere fast. Indeed, as already covered, it is exactly this kind of thinking that results in the depletion of our prefrontal cortex and impairs our ability to concentrate in work more generally.

In many ways, the ethos that sits behind the taking of regular breaks is self-explanatory. We don't even need to look at the wealth of research linking it to enhanced cognition and improved wellbeing (though there will be more on that shortly).

After all, when it comes to our devices (you know, those pesky things causing us so much distraction in the first place) we recognize it's necessary for us to recharge after use. In fact, we know that the more we use them, the faster the battery will deplete. So why don't we recognize the same trait in ourselves? Of course, humans are naturally more complicated and nuanced than technology – but the core of this logic can be applied to the human cognitive system, too. Ultimately, if you don't give your brain time to recharge, it will eventually shut down at an inconvenient, even disastrous, moment.

Still, the evidence for the benefits of work breaks is more than just logic based. Indeed, there is a whole bank of research proving what a positive impact breaks can have on our ability to focus.

Take a study led by William S Helton, a professor of human factors and applied cognition at George Mason

University. Helton's research looked at university students, tasking them with the monitoring of railway maps for a 45-minute period – an exercise which required sustained attention. One group had no breaks, while the other took a five-minute break midway through, engaging in various activities like sitting quietly, listening to music, watching a music video, choosing between music or video, or spending the break as they wished.

Regardless of the break activity, students in the break groups outperformed those who continued without interruption. This study clearly highlights the positive impact of even brief breaks on attention and overall task performance – so next time you claim you don't have time to take a break, remember that, overall, your work is more likely to suffer if you stay on task without break than if you allow yourself some time aside (Rees et al, 2017).

In many ways, we need to reimagine the way we think about our focus altogether, seeing it not as a limitless substance we can continually plunder, but instead recognizing that it is a valuable and limited cognitive resource that is refined and regenerated in periods of mental respite.

Really, our brains are incredibly intricate and complicated machines, and we can't keep endlessly turning the cogs without stopping to oil the machinery from time to time. In this sense, purposeful breaks provide us with an opportunity to reset our neurological wiring – and the more we're able to do this, the better equipped our brains become at weathering stress and sustaining attention in demanding situations.

Still, this fix is not as simple as taking five minutes here and there when things get overwhelming. In fact, the intention and purpose you bring to your break times can have a huge effect on the restorative quality they bring.

It's also important to remember that, implemented correctly, regular breaks are a preventive measure when it comes to burnout – not something you should only indulge when things become too much. At that point, taking a break is about as effective as a sticking plaster on a bullet hole. For this very reason, it's important the breaks we do take are spent truly detached from the work at hand. A clear line must be drawn between the task you're currently tackling and the time you spend away from it.

But you don't need to take my word for it. Research consistently underscores the vital role of regular breaks and psychological detachment from work in promoting focus and productivity. In stressful environments, time away from a task is not always enough, as thoughts of the work worrying us can linger even when it's not directly in front of us. This is why it's so key that we're able to find activities that truly disengage our prefrontal cortex and allow our focus to soften.

A study involving US Forest Service workers revealed that dealing with workplace disrespect led to rumination and insomnia. This really shines a light on the negative consequences work can have, even after we've 'officially' clocked off. Indeed, the same study found that employees who effectively detached after work or engaged in activities like yoga and walking reported fewer sleep problems (Demsky et al, 2019).

Similarly, a review by Sabine Sonnentag also found that workers who were psychologically disconnected during off-hours experienced higher life satisfaction and less psychological strain, without this time in any way compromising their engagement at work. Perhaps unsurprisingly, the same review also found that holidays also provide small but tangible benefits for employees. Sonnentag found that people reported reduced exhaustion, fewer health complaints and increased life satisfaction after time away (Sonnentag, 2012). Even a two-week break among teachers resulted in heightened work engagement and decreased burnout levels, as outlined in a follow-up study.

Still, it is worth noting that these benefits declined a few weeks after employees had returned to work – hence regular daily breaks are necessary to retain the positive effects reported by Sonnentag (Kühnel and Sonnentag, 2010). While it is tempting, sometimes, to believe that a vacation is enough to make up for an onslaught of stress and overwhelm in our daily life, the reality is we need to be able to find a new normal in which stress is a rarity, rather than a near-constant working state.

Now, I know – of course – that for many people taking regular breaks is not as simple as stepping away from work anytime you fancy. Clearly, the demands to be at our desk are often intense, and given what we've already discussed about the self-sustaining nature of toxic work cultures, regular breaks have the potential to trigger resentment in colleagues. This is why I would always first suggest that – where possible – micro-breaks be incorporated primarily as a change in workplace culture.

If you are a leader or higher up, this change can come from you. Ideally, it should be structured and intentional – that means having explicit conversations with colleagues about taking more breaks, with a clear suggestion of how this might look day to day. In order for such shifts in work culture to stick, there need to be well-drawn boundaries regarding what is expected, as well as wiggle room to adapt when issues do come up. Remember, take feedback, but also ensure that whatever pattern of breaks you agree on, they are pre-scheduled with a fixed timestamp so that they don't overrun past the point of being advantageous.

Equally, for those without the seniority to implement such a change themselves, conversations at work can still be worth having. I've seen major structural changes begin because of changes within just one small team. Sceptical as people may be, the proof is in the pudding – and when people start performing better thanks to regular breaks, it's not long before others want to follow suit. Given the wealth of evidence that sits behind the theory, you certainly have an auspicious starting point for winning colleagues and senior team members over. Still, even in situations where this is not possible, there is scope to reap the benefit of regular breaks on an individual level.

After all, regular breaks don't always have to require a dramatic change of scenery to be effective. What's more important is that you're able to do your best to move your mind away from the demands of your immediate 'to do' list. That means you must try your hardest to resist the temptation to scroll social media.

We'll discuss in more detail in Chapter 8 what desk-side activities might be beneficial for brief, micro-breaks – but first, I must put forward another crucial part of the equation to achieve more by doing less. And that (surprise, surprise!) is daydreaming.

Burning bright, not out – the creative edge

By now, you probably already know how I feel about creativity. To me, this is not a fluffy nice-to-have but an essential and enduring life skill that should be exercised on a daily basis. There are a number of reasons for this, many of them obvious, but there is also a broader reason you may not be so privy to – and that is the power of creativity to change the way in which we live and approach our routine.

We sometimes have a rather narrow view of creativity. We tend to think of it in the same terms as more general work, that it's something we engage in at a specific time – and that it ends the moment we stop putting it into direct practice. But this is not the case. In many ways, there's good reason to think of creativity more as a state of mind. It can manifest specifically during occasions such as brainstorming sessions, yes, but it can also be present in our attitude and the decisions we make about how we approach and organize our life.

This is why learning to live with an attitude of creativity offers such huge benefits – both on the granular level but also with the big-picture stuff. One study showed that in design students, a 'growth' creative mindset (that is, a mindset in which the person believes their own creativity can grow and expand) is associated with a positive attitude towards tasks, as well as more enjoyment derived from completing those tasks (Puente-Díaz and Cavazos-Arroyo, 2017). In other words, faith in your own creative ability can improve your mood and motivation, as well as the quality of your work.

When you are functioning at a higher creative level, you start to see things from a new perspective. This is after all one of the fundamental qualities of original thinking – seeing potential for novelty and unconventional solutions that are practically invisible when operating from a more conventional outlook. This quality is one that can be hugely beneficial to the general efficacy of your work. It enables an individual to work through problems faster, navigate complexity with clarity, and even redesign their routine in a way that bolsters output and enjoyment.

I hope, then, that we are in agreement that being able to embrace creativity is something that will enable you to improve your work, while also boosting mood and overall success. So, then, what does this have to do with breaks? Well, that's a good question. Given that – as already covered – regular breaks help to foster the resilience of the prefrontal cortex, we already know that this is a beneficial habit that can improve productivity and help stave off stress. But consider, too, that daydreaming offers the added advantage of enhanced creativity and mental clarity – and it's not hard to see why combining these two things is something of a no-brainer.

As mentioned in Chapter 4, a study undertaken in 2012 examined participants engaging in demanding tasks and observed their performance with and without daydreaming breaks. The results indicated that mind-wandering during breaks was associated with increased productivity, something which – given similar research indicating the productive benefits of even more general breaks – clearly compounds the overall productivity impact (Baird et al, 2012).

What's more, other research indicates that mind wandering is crucial to creative incubation, allowing the brain to disengage from the linear confines of the focused mind. Josh Davis, director of research at the NeuroLeadership Institute, highlights in the *Harvard Business Review* that maintaining an 'always on' approach can impede productivity by hindering the brain processes that occur during moments of wandering thoughts. He points out that the digital age, with its constant information influx from devices, has further eroded the potential benefits of creative incubation by preventing individuals from experiencing the restful and inspirational states that daydreaming can induce (Davis, 2015). Put another way, allowing the mind to wander during breaks is more than vaguely beneficial – it might actually be instrumental to unlocking creativity and problem-solving capacities that would otherwise remain dormant in a hyper-connected work environment.

Daydreaming might also help with that resource that can be so evasive in overwhelming work cultures: motivation. Research from the University of Western Australia sheds an interesting light on the visual-based nature of motivational inspiration. The study found that individuals who vividly imagined themselves engaging in an activity were more inspired to work compared to those simply told to work. Dr Ji, the researcher behind the study, suggests that pre-experiencing the most rewarding moments of an activity through visualization boosts motivation. This heightened motivation acts as a catalyst for greater productivity (News Medical, 2021).

Of course, this might sound counterintuitive to the advice that breaks should enable you to remove yourself from a working environment – but for me, it seems to speak to the breadth of potential that daydreaming can provide. Sometimes, it will feel best to allow our thoughts to roam far away from the demands of the present moment – while at other points, we might find it more helpful to envision the rewards of a task well done in order to source motivation.

Deciding which option is best for you is just another benefit of focused daydreaming. Done regularly and consistently, it allows us to better tune into how we're feeling – bringing more awareness to our overall energy levels so we might act in a way that aligns with the way our brain and body feels. That is another reason 'intentional' is such a key word here. So much of the problem with the current work culture is a lack of awareness; we simply get thrown around in the tide of continuous stress and busyness.

This is why combining regular breaks with the act of focused daydreaming has the power to be truly transformative. It gives our brains the mental space to keep our train of thought running smoothly, our motivation topped up, our outlook positive, and – most importantly of all – our overall creative abilities sharp and present.

So, yes, on the surface taking more breaks to achieve more might sound like a bizarre recipe for work success. But in practice, making a daily habit of focused daydreaming might just allow you to reach new productive heights without any of the associated downsides of exhaustion and burnout.

Knowing the burnout signs

So, it's fair to say we can all agree that burnout is something we want to avoid, but what actually is burnout and how does it affect not only our mental state, but our bodies too? It is clear that the biggest threat to our working lives, and maybe even our lives in general, is stress.

We all deal with stress differently, and likewise stress manifests in our bodies in different ways. For example, a couple of years after launching the successful media empire Huffington Post, editor-in-chief Arianna Huffington reported being so run down from running her business that she collapsed on her desk, breaking her cheekbone and almost losing an eye (Michel, 2016). Now, you may be thinking – how did she let her exhaustion reach that limit? But often we do not realize how big our tornado of stress has become until we've already been whipped away in it. Of course, it may not always be as serious as losing an eye. It may just be that you've realized that, due to stress, you keep saying no to social events and now you never seem to get an invite. Either way, you're giving something up because you're exhausting your body and leaving yourself too burned out to function.

Indeed, Huffington is not alone when it comes to stress causing physical harm to her body, as many others reported crashing from overworking too. It is obvious, then, that burnout is not just a mental state, but can actually take a significant physical toll that extends beyond our work life. These are the consequences of an overly demanding work culture that drives us to stress and therefore burnout with sometimes devastating consequences. We must, then, acknowledge burnout as a real condition, one that leaves its mark on both the brain and the body.

German-born US psychologist Herbert J Freudenberger was one of the first to explore the concept of staff burnout in 1974, with many considering him the 'founding father' of the concept. He studied the physical strains and behavioural indicators that came with burnout, and it is he who made the term 'burnout' popular in a number of science publications. Although he did not invent the term, he did use it to describe the mental condition he and his colleagues had been experiencing under serious stress, hence how the term 'burnout' became a workplace condition linked to stress.

In an article in 1974, around the time he coined the expression, Freudenberger described burnout as 'becoming exhausted by making excessive demands on energy, strength or resources in the workplace' (Heinemann and Heinemann, 2017). He noted that some symptoms of burnout include fatigue, exhaustion, headaches, sleeplessness, anger and depression. He also noted how burnout can lead to use of drugs such as tranquillizers. It's worth noting that all of the symptoms listed by Freudenberger are not just mental symptoms, but physical ones too. It is a reminder that, even 60 years ago, burnout was considered a real condition – and today we're only more aware of its prevalence.

So, burnout is a condition that affects our mental health and, in some cases, our physical health, but how does it affect our brains? Psychologists at the Karolinska Institutet in Sweden provided evidence that workplace-related burnout can interfere with neural circuits, causing a vicious cycle of neurological dysfunction (Michel, 2016). For example, research led by Armita Golkar et al (2014) resulted in an experiment that involved 40 participants who had been diagnosed with burnout. All participants explained their burnout came from a stressful working environment in which they worked long hours each week for many years. Golkar also found 70 'healthy' people who had not been formally diagnosed with burnout or stress. Each group took part in two test sessions, one of which was a task that measured their ability to regulate negative emotions and another that evaluated their brain's connectivity using resting-state functional MRI (R-fMRI). Participants were shown a series of neutral and negative emotional images to assess their reactions to stress.

The image would stay on screen for five seconds before a set of instructions would appear, telling each participant to either suppress, intensify or maintain their emotional response to the picture. After this instruction, the image would appear on the screen again for another five seconds, and a loud startling sound played. As the sound played, an electrode taped to the participant's cheek would record their reactions. When the two groups were asked to maintain or intensify their emotions, the responses were similar. However, when they were asked to suppress their emotional responses, the group who had experienced burnout reported more difficulty in controlling their negative emotional responses in comparison to the 'healthy' participants.

Now, this is where it gets interesting. The differences in the brain between the burnout group and the 'healthy' group appeared mainly in the amygdala. The amygdala is a small, almond-shaped structure tucked into the central part of your brain. It is part of a larger network inside the brain called the limbic system (Cleveland Clinic, 2023).

The amygdala and the limbic system are extremely important when it comes to our survival. It was found that participants in the burnout group had an enlarged amygdala, as well as significantly weaker connections between the amygdala and other areas of the brain linked to emotional distress, such as the anterior cingulate cortex. The anterior cingulate cortex is the front-most portion of the cingulate cortex and is involved in several complex, higher-level cognitive functions, such as impulse control, emotion and decision making. The more stressed the participant felt, the weaker the connectivity between the amygdala and the anterior cingulate cortex appeared on the R-fMRI (Michel, 2016). It was also shown that there were weaker correlations between activity in the amygdala and the medial prefrontal cortex in the burnout group. The medial prefrontal cortex is involved in the orchestration of thoughts and actions in accordance with goals.

In another experiment, Ivanka Savic measured participants' degree of burnout and the toll of physical stress. The results found that burnout leaves a big mark on the amygdala, anterior cingulate cortex, and the medial prefrontal cortex. The frontal cortex, an area of the brain that is essential to cognitive function, begins to thin as we age, but participants who had suffered from burnout showed a more pronounced thinning of their frontal cortex.

Other effects of ageing were also shown to be more prominent. Savic says that there is a vicious cycle in which the amygdala overreacts which impairs the medial prefrontal cortex, which leads back to the amygdala over-reacting further and so on. As this cycle continues, brain structures start to tarnish, leading to horrible cognitive effects such as memory, emotional and attention difficulties. All this is to say, burnout is not just a state of stress that can be cured by a quick vacation. It is a condition that can have long-lasting effects on your brain's ability to function and can even speed the brain's ageing process. Of course, I do not say this to stoke fear, but to stress the importance of engaging in an activity that offers protection from this state. It's exciting that, given the prominence of this condition, there is actually a tool that can provide real respite from it!

Summary: do less, achieve more!

In this chapter we have delved into a fun paradox: achieving more by doing less. We challenge the conventional wisdom that perpetual busyness is the hallmark of productivity. At the core of this exploration is a critique of the entrenched Busy Fool Syndrome (BFS) that dominates the workplace. By advocating for a fundamental paradigm shift, we urge you to step back from the precipice of ceaseless toil and reconsider how true productivity can be achieved through strategic, mindful engagement with our work.

Central to this re-evaluation is an understanding of how our brains operate under stress and the detrimental impact of BFS on our cognitive functions, particularly within the prefrontal cortex. The neuroscientific underpinnings of stress and its ramifications underscore a poignant truth: the way we work under the scourge of BFS not only hampers our productivity, but also erodes our mental and physical health.

Offering a pathway out of BFS, we can see the obvious virtues of focused daydreaming and regular, purposeful breaks as vehicles for rejuvenating our mental state and, by extension, enhancing our creative and productive capabilities. Far from advocating idleness, the call to embrace strategic breaks is a bid to recognize and operationalize the neuroscientific fact that our brains need time to recharge to function optimally. This is not merely about stepping away from our desks but about recalibrating our approach to work to foster an environment where creativity can flourish.

By challenging the glorified hustle culture, we advocate for a reimagined ethos of work where success is measured not by the hours we put in but by the wisdom with which we allocate our energy and time. This chapter invites you to consider how incorporating intentional breaks and fostering daydreaming can not only enhance your work output but also enrich your professional life with greater creativity and satisfaction.

CHAPTER SIX

Reconnect with your curious mind!

The human brain is like a sponge. Even when you're not aware of it, it is continually processing a wide range of experiences and stimuli – it is always learning and adapting, adding more data to its memory banks and broadening your own, personal understanding of the world that surrounds you.

While most of us know and accept that this is happening, it's not something we have to really think about. In fact, technically it's not something that requires any input from us whatsoever. There can certainly be a conscious element to the way we encode memories – for instance, paying attention to the route we're taking when walking around a new city or environment – but there is still so much we absorb without having to set an intention to do so. That's because the magic is happening out of the sight of our conscious mind.

Most of us are aware that non-conscious levels of the mind exist. Even so, these non-conscious portions are primarily conceptual to us. By definition, we are not aware of what we're not aware of. It feels to us that our mind starts and ends with all that we have conscious access to. Yet, you also know that you have access to knowledge you are not directly thinking about in any given moment.

For example, if prompted, you could recall a childhood memory, or access other facets of knowledge, whether they be basic facts or complex learnings taken from your education. That's because this information is stored in the subconscious. It may not be illuminated by the light of your awareness at all times, but it only takes the briefest spark of intent to flip on the lights and you can access what's there.

In popular culture, the terms 'subconscious' and 'unconscious' are often thrown around interchangeably, but they are actually distinct facets that make up the whole – even though there isn't always unanimous agreement amongst psychologists about the boundaries between the two. Perhaps the most famous analogy for the conscious, subconscious and unconscious mind comes from Sigmund Freud.

Freud proposed that these three areas of the mind are much like an iceberg. Our conscious mind is like the tip of the iceberg, clearly visible to us but only making up a small portion of the full structure of the mind; our subconscious – or 'preconscious' – is the portion just below the surface, which can be seen from above but is obscured by the water; while our unconscious is the very bottom of the iceberg, shrouded in darkness, an important part of the whole but not at all visible from the surface (Mcleod, 2009).

For the purposes of this chapter, we will use the following definitions for the different parts of the mind:

- **The conscious mind**. The conscious mind is the part of the mind that is aware of and focused on current thoughts, feelings, perceptions and experiences. It is the mental state that you are actively aware of at any given moment.

- **The subconscious mind**. The subconscious mind is the part of the mind that operates below the level of conscious awareness. It holds information, memories and automatic processes that influence thoughts, behaviours and emotions without the individual being fully aware of them. Though not constantly in view, you might still draw on the information here when needed, bringing it into your conscious awareness.

- **The unconscious mind**. The unconscious mind refers to the deepest part of the mind that contains thoughts, memories and desires that are beyond the reach of your conscious awareness. It includes elements that may be repressed or unknown to the individual and can influence behaviour and emotions in subtle ways.

You may be wondering by this point why exactly any of this matters. Well, the answer lies in the nature of creativity itself. As we have already covered, there is a tendency in culture to think about creativity as something mystical or hard to pin down. Part of the reason for this is the way we form ideas in the first place. While it's true that we can generate ideas when tasked with doing so, often our best ones come to us seemingly at random. It's perhaps unsurprising, then, that the subconscious mind plays a key role in our creative ability.

It can often be hard to define or even agree on exactly what creativity is. The slippery nature of ideas and originality – as well as its many applications – only add to its generalized obfuscation. In terms of its etymology, the word 'creativity' is derived from a Latin word, *creo*, which means to make or create something (Fohtung, 2016). Really, at its core, this is all creativity is: the creation of something new.

It's worth noting, of course, that this doesn't have to mean creating something in a literal sense. Yes, creativity might manifest as an invention or a work of art, but it could also be the creation of a new perspective or novel solution to a difficult problem. In other words, creativity is a vast and varied thing. Indeed, its agility is what makes it so wonderful. We can be creative in big and small ways, whether that's as simple as coming up with a clever short-cut home, or conceiving an idea for a game-changing new project.

Originality is another interesting concept you'll frequently hear mentioned in the same breath as creativity. It is assumed that true creativity must also be original. The online Cambridge Dictionary defines originality as 'The quality of being special and interesting and not the same as anything or anyone else' (Cambridge Dictionary, 2019). Certainly, this definition gives us some food for thought. Most of us tend to think of an original idea as something completely new, but this isn't entirely accurate. In many ways, 'special' and 'interesting' are more useful terms when it comes to considering what we might genuinely label as original.

This is because, to some extent, we can't ever create anything truly new. Creativity is really the act of combining existing knowledge and/or ideas to create something that has the appearance of novelty. Think of it this way – we might call an artist 'original' even though they're not capable of inventing a new colour. Instead, we recognize that the way they've blended shades, the different materials they've used and the techniques they've applied together have the compound effect of seeming novel or interesting.

The same rules apply to us in work and day-to-day life. Ostensibly, this might seem a lesson in the limits of creativity – but actually, it's the opposite. There are an infinite number of ways we might combine subjects or ideas to take us in new, exciting directions. Even just one good idea might eventually lay the groundwork for a thousand more – imagine if the invention of the wheel had ended with carts and wagons, rather than paving the way for everything from motorcars to aeroplanes and everything else that has come since.

As Steve Jobs once said, 'creativity is just connecting things' – what's more, as Jobs points out, ask someone how exactly they came up with an idea and they'll look a little guilty. This, he notes, is because 'they didn't really do it, they just saw something' (Farnham Street, 2014).

And this is the rub. It is our subconscious that receives vast amounts of data from the world around us. In many ways, it is the sorting room of our mind. This is also why it's the creative centre of the brain, running hypotheses you aren't aware of and combining seemingly unrelated pieces of information. It is also the subconscious mind which becomes activated when we daydream. And so, in order to make the most of this raw creative power, we need to learn to harness this portion of the mind so we can direct our innovative thinking in a helpful direction.

Subconscious feng shui

We are living in an age in which content is abundant. Even that word – 'content' – might refer to a plethora of things in our modern moment. In many ways, today, everything is content. From news articles to videos on social media, we are in the constant presence of ideas, people and information. As already mentioned, there are doubtless many benefits to this. Our every curiosity and stray thought can be satisfied at the drop of a hat (or, more accurately, the drop of a search engine). Yet, this onslaught of never-ending stuff can also be pretty overwhelming.

Few of us would say that everything that enters our field of awareness is hugely mentally enriching. In many cases, it might even be actively distracting. Consider, too, that the fast-moving nature of entertainment and content in the modern world spells bad news for our attention span, and it's clear that what we're most regularly filling our subconscious up with is random, fragmented intel that really isn't all that useful to us.

Of course, no one is suggesting we should censor and monitor all the information we encounter day-to-day

– doing so would likely be logistically impossible, anyway – but instead, that we must recognize that the quality and content of what we put in our head naturally has a knock-on effect on our thinking. This, in turn, has an impact on the quality of our ideas and the positioning of our overall mindset.

Think of it this way... a friend comes to you complaining of frequent nightmares. Then, in the next breath, they tell you about their new routine of binge-watching horror films just before bedtime. You'd surely advise them that perhaps their viewing habits are having a knock-on effect on the dreams they're then experiencing when sleeping. Yet, when people today complain that their creativity feels lacking, or that their attention is quick to tire, we don't seem to connect these things to all that we are viewing, watching and reading throughout the course of an average day.

That's why what I am about to tell you next is so crucial to finding success as a focused daydreamer. You've likely heard the saying, 'tidy kitchen, tidy mind' – similarly, most of us have had the experience of feeling our productivity increase after clearing up our workstation. Well, by the same logic, that's why we need to 'feng shui' the cluttered room of our subconscious mind in order to truly harness the benefits of focused daydreaming.

Appropriately enough, in the Chinese tradition, feng shui relates to the arrangement of a room and the subsequent flow of energies. This is actually a very fitting metaphor for how we might better organize our subconscious brain so that it can direct its creative energies in a productive and illuminating way. When we daydream, our focused mind gets a rest – but our subconscious powers up. The link between the daydreaming mind and the brain's default network is such that it is during these periods of reflection that we're able to engage in passive sensory processing.

This is because our brain uses mind-wandering moments to work through visual processing in such a way that we can appreciate aesthetic beauty, engage in semantic processing in order to encode language (written or spoken) with meaning, and even process our emotions (and the emotions of others) via our limbic system.

To describe this another way, from a neurological perspective, engaging our default network is what provides our subconscious with the raw materials it can then use to get creative. This is important for a number of reasons. One reason is that, when we're not allowing our brain to enter this state often enough, we are short-changing our subconscious. The other is that the material we are – often inadvertently – inputting then has a direct correlation with our own creative output (or lack thereof).

Returning to the artist metaphor for a moment, we might think of the subconscious as a supplier of tools and inspiration. After all, even the best artist will struggle to produce good work when not provided with a canvas, brush or paints to work with. Equally, they will struggle to get started if they lack a starting idea to prompt them to actually put these tools into action. So often people blame this creative dearth on themselves, assuming they are simply not 'creative' enough – when in reality they are not supplying themselves with the raw materials and momentum needed to make this creative output possible.

So, what to do about it all? It is no good taking up focused daydreaming if you're not also going to pay attention to what you're inputting into your personal brain box. Like putting the wrong kind of fuel in your car, you might be able to sputter along for a bit, but you're not going to be reaching the speeds or distances you're actually capable of.

That's why taking time to read, research and otherwise acquaint yourself with the areas you'd most like to apply yourself in is a key part of the focused daydreaming process. A bit like stretching before working out, this is what allows us to expand our mind, build resilience and lay the foundation for ongoing success.

The beauty of why!

Anyone who has small children – or indeed, anyone who has been around them in any capacity – will tell you that kids have an irrepressible sense of curiosity. To them, the world is new, and they are very keen to learn all about it. There is almost no fact, observation or revelation which can't elicit another 'why?' when talking to a child.

It's no coincidence, either, that children are so full of creative energy. The novelty of the world keeps their minds sharp, while the organic neuroplasticity associated with younger brains allows them to tap into vast resources of bright imagination. Sadly, as we age, most of us lose this sense of wonder at the world. We become ossified, naturally acclimatized to our environment, and in doing so the things that would have once sparked our curiosity simply fade into the background.

What's more, this is only worsened by the current state of Busy Fool Syndrome (BFS). When we're embroiled in stressful environments with constant demands on our time and attention, there is little wiggle room for things we might otherwise be interested in to grab our attention. A stressed mind is so often also a static mind; wilted and depleted, the burned-out brain no longer seeks the nourishing light of learning.

This is bad news for our subconscious. Inquisitiveness is a great and natural driver of learning. In fact, research suggests that curiosity lays a sturdy foundation for real, substantive education – allowing us to retain more, and also making the process of encoding that information more enjoyable (Blue, 2022). This is why I believe it is vitally important that we reconnect with the curious mind. After all, if curiosity improves our learning, it also necessarily improves the quality of the materials we provide our subconscious with.

Let's go back to our artist metaphor again. When tasked with producing a collage, an artist will naturally be able to produce something better with higher-quality photographs than pixelated prints – and so it is that the better quality our learning, the more creative scope there is for our default network to get busy with this information. Embracing your curious mind is a great way to immediately boost the quality of your ideas, and also the frequency with which they come up. In other words, it allows you to fuel up your subconscious so that it's well supplied with paint, pastels, brushes, canvases – and anything else it might require to produce a masterpiece.

Well, if curiosity is the key – we simply need to be more curious. Easy enough right? Except how do you actually reconnect with that curiosity when your natural child-like wonder sometimes seems to belong to a past life? Well, worry not, for I have a full – though certainly not exhaustive – list of how you can do exactly that.

Ways to boost your curiosity

Ask 'why' more

Sometimes it really is that simple. Now, no one is suggesting you take this as a licence to behave like a preschooler, launching an incessant stream of questions at everyone around you (though, who knows, perhaps this could lead to some interesting conversations!).

Instead, this is something that can be practised both individually and in opportune moments with others. We all still carry inside us a natural flame of curiosity – this is one of the innate and immovable qualities of being human – we just need to recapture the flair for fanning that flame again. Asking 'why?' more frequently is one of the simplest and most effective ways of doing just that.

Sometimes this might be a private endeavour. Follow your instincts. Maybe you feel the slightest whisper of curiosity while, for example, commuting into work on the train. This might appear in any form: a question about how wind turbines work after spotting one through the window, or a flicker of interest in the subject of a book you've noticed someone else reading. Instead of allowing that wave of curiosity to ebb and dissipate without recognition, act on it!

After all, we do have access to a whole world of information at our fingertips via our devices – we might as well use it to our benefit more often. Better still, you might be able to engage in conversation with someone and hear more from them directly. Asking a stranger if they're enjoying the book they're reading might seem like a small gesture, but the creative rewards might just be massive.

As an added bonus, learning to ask why can also be a helpful salve to BFS. We so often take on new work without considering whether it's appropriate or timely. 'Why?' is an effective starting point for helping us to reject work we don't have the time for – as well as a way of approaching what we do have to do with more strategy.

It's just one little question, but the impact of asking why more might just lead you down roads you never could have anticipated – and reawaken your curiosity in the process.

Start seeing again

Once upon a time, the world seemed rich and vibrant. On every corner there was a new thing to discover. Now, the mundane is invisible – in fact, even the exciting can become unremarkable through the drudgery of familiarity. Cheesy as it may be, there really is beauty all around if you take the time to look for it. Watch how a toddler interacts with this world and it will become readily apparent; stopping to inspect the white fluff of dandelions, beaming up at the electric blue of the sky. It's not impossible for us to recapture some of this wonder.

But how? Well, the first step is to start seeing again. In many ways this could be viewed as an act of mindfulness. Rather than letting your surroundings wash over you without real thought or note, take time to notice what you're seeing. At the start, this often works best when you pick a particular time of day you can always practise the action. That might be while out on a walk, or even staring out of the window as you do the washing up.

If you're struggling to keep your attention on what's in front of you, try listing what you can see – better still, note one quality about every single thing you see. It doesn't have to be anything profound, it could simply be a colour, texture or other observation. The real idea is to start turning up your awareness so you can rediscover what surrounds you, connect with it, and by doing so re-spark your own curiosity. After all, it's hard to follow your natural curiosity when you're blind to what's going on – but learning to see again all the interesting things that surround you is a great way to reconnect with your natural inquisitiveness.

Follow the thoughts

Have you ever thought about the pattern of your thoughts? We often don't pay attention to the ways thoughts rise and form in our mind, especially as we usually fly through them so quickly. By the time we've acknowledged one thought, we're already moving on to the next. Really, this is a shallow form of thinking. Stressed and overburdened as we often are, we rarely allow ourselves the pleasure of burrowing into ideas or topics we find truly interesting. Instead, we get caught up in the surface-level buzz and stress that keeps us anxious and occupied by all the imminent tasks we need to tackle.

While following your thoughts might sound like a risk when it comes to overthinking, the trick is learning which thoughts to give momentum to – and which to leave idle. Really, this is actually an excellent way to engage in daydreaming itself. Our mind is a natural connection-making machine. If you find yourself remembering an old interest, why not let those thoughts spring new ones? This kind of introspection is exactly the kind of thing we're missing from day-to-day life when tangled up in the minutia of working life.

Welcome discomfort

It's not perhaps what everyone wants to hear, but discomfort can be of great value for a number of reasons. We're not talking, of course, about sitting on a bed of nails or otherwise inflicting random discomforts on yourself. Instead, this is about getting out of your comfort zone (yes, that old chestnut!). Certainly, we receive so many messages in the media and culture about the benefits of being bold and brave that we sometimes become immune to the truth behind the message.

In real terms, being told to actively seek discomfort is sort of annoying. Life can seem hard enough as it is without us needing to add anything else on top. Here's the catch, though: as hard a pill as it might be to swallow, getting outside your comfort zone also brings great rewards. It also naturally promotes curiosity. In fact, curiosity can be a great way to summon the bravery required to embrace this kind of discomfort.

It's worth noting, too, that this doesn't have to mean taking up an extreme sport or tackling a phobia that genuinely terrifies you. Instead, it's about taking on the small things you'd usually avoid – and looking for more opportunities to do just that. For example, that might be joining a class to learn a new language, or reading a book on a topic you'd usually find too intimidating.

It's even something you can practise in the workplace. Find someone who does something different to you and actually try and understand their role. These little baby steps out of your comfort zone can whet your curiosity to discover more, uncover new experiences, and generally awaken you to the creative power of being a little more inquisitive.

Good ideas don't happen in the boardroom

Now you know just how clear the connection is between what you put your focus on and what your subconscious can then use to be creative with, you can bring more intention and awareness to the process. As I've said, this does not necessarily mean that you are overcautious of everything that you're putting into your head – instead it's about taking time to give your subconscious the materials you'd like it to get innovative with. Of course, switching off afterwards and taking time to actively daydream is also a key part of this process.

Perhaps the easiest example of how to apply this method is when you're faced with a complex problem at work. While it might be tempting to try and think of solutions in the moment, it will actually be more beneficial to you to reacquaint yourself with the problem without feeling the need to force the answers. This actually takes the pressure away from you, but also still gives you the information you need for when your default mode network comes online (Crawford, 2022). By doing this, you give your subconscious the materials it needs to try and unpick the problem and throw up novel solutions. You'll find most complex problems encountered in business are not solved when brainstorming in a boardroom! In short, daydreaming is your sports car – and by taking the time to fuel up your subconscious you can ensure it is running at top speed, in great condition!

> *Without leaps of imagination, or dreaming,*
> *we lose the excitement of possibilities.*
> *Dreaming, after all, is a form of planning.*
> GLORIA STEINEM, AMERICAN POLITICAL ACTIVIST AND AUTHOR

What do we miss when rushing?

In a Washington DC metro station, on a cold January morning in 2007, a man with a violin played six Bach pieces for about 45 minutes. During that time, approximately 1,100 people went through the station, most of them on their way to work.

After about three minutes, a middle-aged man noticed that there was a musician playing. He slowed his pace and stopped for a few seconds, and then hurried on to meet his schedule. About four minutes later, the violinist received his first dollar. A woman threw money in the hat and, without stopping, continued to walk. At six minutes, a young man leaned against the wall to listen to him, then looked at his watch and started to walk again.

At 10 minutes, a three-year-old boy stopped, but his mother tugged him along hurriedly. The boy stopped to look at the violinist again, but the mother pulled hard and the child continued to walk, turning his head the whole time. This action was repeated by several other children, but every parent – without exception – forced their children to move on quickly.

At 45 minutes, the musician had been playing continuously. Only six people had stopped and listened for a short while. About 20 had given him money but had continued to walk at their normal pace. The man collected a total of $32. After one hour, he finished playing and silence took over. No one noticed and no one applauded. There was no recognition at all.

No one knew this, but the violinist was Joshua Bell, one of the greatest musicians in the world. He played one of the most intricate pieces ever written, with a violin worth $3.5 million. Three days earlier, Joshua Bell had sold out a theatre in Boston where the seats averaged $100 each to sit and listen to him play the same music.

This is a true story. Joshua Bell playing incognito in the DC metro station was organized by the *Washington Post* as part of a social experiment about 'perception, taste and people's priorities'.

This experiment raised several questions. In a commonplace environment, at an inappropriate hour, do we still perceive beauty? And if so, do we stop to appreciate it? Do we recognize talent in an unexpected context? One possible conclusion from this experiment could be this: if we do not have a moment to stop and listen to one of the best musicians in the world, playing some of the finest music ever written, with one of the most beautiful instruments ever made... how many other things are we missing as we rush through life (Weingarten, 2007)?

What more reason do you need to always maintain your curiosity? To pay attention to what you see, hear, smell, touch or taste? When we breeze through life we lose so much. Make more time for idling now and then.

Summary: sculpting creativity

Curiosity is the putty with which creativity is sculpted. As we have explored, the human brain is akin to a sponge, always ready to soak up new experiences and stimuli, even when we are not consciously aware of it. By exploring different facets of our mind – conscious, subconscious and unconscious – we have developed a deeper understanding of how we encode experiences and memories.

We've discovered that our mind is not restricted to our conscious thoughts. It goes much deeper, storing memories and behavioural influences at the subconscious and unconscious levels. The information and insights lying in these regions aren't actively in our thoughts, yet can be activated by a sudden spark of intent, shedding light on forgotten or overlooked areas of life and creativity.

We've delved into the phenomenon of creativity, picking apart its nebulous nature and pinpointing a more concrete definition. Creativity isn't an abstract concept or a magical elixir but simply the act of creating something new – a new perspective, a novel solution, an original method.

We have also busted some myths about originality, helping us to see that it is not necessarily about 'true' uniqueness, but rather about presenting things in fresh, interesting ways. Our thinking is shaped and limited by what we have already encountered, making the act of combining old knowledge in new and innovative ways a core tenet of creativity. It's by feeding our subconscious mind with quality, intentional content that we can encourage the synthesis of truly original ideas, despite the environmental data to which we are constantly exposed.

We've clarified the need to 'feng shui' the cluttered room of our subconscious mind, making it a more conducive environment for fostering creativity in the areas we choose. By being purposeful with the content that fills our minds, we can enhance our creative output and overall mindset, optimizing the alignment between our inputs and those outputs that are truly meaningful and beneficial.

We've gained insights into how to effectively boost our curiosity through simple yet practical methods such as asking 'why' more, intentionally observing our surroundings, and embracing a little discomfort here and there. The ultimate goal is to step outside our comfort zones, embracing a spirit of adventure and inquisitiveness that fuels our innate, human curiosity.

As we apply these insights in our day-to-day lives, problem solving doesn't have to be a push-and-pull process. It can be an exhilarating joy ride with our subconscious at the wheel and our conscious mind in the passenger seat where it belongs, secure in the knowledge that this journey into the unknown is powered by the fuel of wonder and driven by the engine of imagination.

CHAPTER SEVEN

Productive mind wandering

When we don't take something seriously, we're much less likely to engage with it meaningfully. It's not exactly hard to grasp why this is the case. Respect is integral to giving a subject the consideration and attentiveness it deserves. This, of course, might refer to any number of things – whether that's trying a new hobby or making plans to reach a new goal. And so it also is with focused daydreaming.

We can recognize, for example, the difference between someone making an offhand comment about wanting to learn a new language and someone who actually starts a class and buys textbooks in pursuit of that goal. Taking something seriously means embracing the positives, but also keeping your eyes open to the challenges. In the example I've just given, if the same person were to flippantly declare that they think learning a language will be easy, you'd likely be sceptical about their ability to see it through. And rightly so.

We know that positivity must also be tempered by realism. Someone might recognize that learning a language comes with a whole host of cognitive benefits, as well as the rewards of practical application, but it is only if they're able to utilize this knowledge to inspire action in themselves that they'll actually achieve the end goal. Really, they need to be aware, ahead of time, of the obstacles they might face (whether that be the niggly particulars of grammar or the challenges of correct pronunciation) so they can keep a grip on their perseverance and ultimately see the whole thing through. We can't shortcut our way out of dedication. The same thing goes for focused daydreaming.

As you're certainly aware by this point in the book, daydreaming isn't really something we take seriously at a societal level. Seriousness is reserved for the things we think are more 'traditionally' business-like – whether that be our professional performance or the way we behave in an important work meeting. That's why I think it's vitally important we do not conflate seriousness with sombreness. After all, a sense of play and imagination are the exact qualities that make mind wandering such a profound creative tool. We must give mind wandering the earnestness it deserves, but also preserve the natural joy and fun that comes along with it.

So, what exactly does taking it seriously look like? Well, it means respecting it – first and foremost. It also means showing discernment. Think of it this way: presented with a child's painting, you'll likely offer praise as you understand this is just a bit of creative expression that doesn't have broader consequences. Yet, if you were to hire an interior designer and found they'd gone off the rails decorating your house in an abstract way, you'd likely complain. We know, in other words, that in a more serious context we must exercise a higher level of judgement.

A key part of discernment is the attempt to find objectivity. It might be tempting to throw this book down, indulge in a bit of mind wandering now and then, and leave it there. But this is not enough if you're serious about reconnecting with your focus and finding a way to restore the cognitive resilience that will enable you to find a real, repeatable path to creative success.

The truth is, to make focused daydreaming work in a serious way, you need to dedicate yourself to it as you would a new lifestyle – taking the same tack you might while trying to eat healthily or implement a new exercise routine. That means no setting over-the-top goals and instead finding a way to fit it into your daily routine while still maintaining a balance with all the other demands on your time and energy.

Of course, building that routine in the first place is an important part of achieving this – but another key element is learning to distinguish, within the realm of your own head, the difference between productive mind wandering and other types of thinking that may be less beneficial. This book clearly aims to champion mind wandering as a creative technique, but it would be doing a disservice to the power of focused daydreaming if we didn't also address the types of mind-wandering that are not so enriching. It would be dishonest, in other words, to only look at the good bits. Yet, in acknowledging the unhealthy forms of daydreaming that also exist, we can also better learn to avoid them.

Not all forms of daydreaming were created equal. We'll dive into the specifics of maladaptive daydreaming – an unhealthy form of mind wandering that should be avoided. But we'll also take a look at how focused daydreaming can improve our cognitive abilities through the strengthening of memory, as well as the science that sits behind it. We will also look at other similar mental techniques – such as mindfulness and meditation – and how they differ from focused daydreaming. With this fuller picture in view, you can make sure you're embracing the powerful aspects of focused daydreaming and using this technique to its fullest advantage.

Away with the fairies

Away with the fairies. Head in the clouds. Lost in thought… these are just a few of the phrases we have for describing when a person has completely zoned out. In French, they have a nice idiom for this, too – *être dans la lune* – literally meaning 'to be in the moon'. I like this one in particular, because when we're on the crest of a particularly vivid daydream, it really can feel like we've left the planet. It's a testament, really, to the power of the human mind – that in a single moment the whole of reality can melt away, leaving us adrift in the rich estuary of our imagination.

Inevitably, getting lost in an elaborate daydream is something we have all done from time to time. In fact, it's something we will all do again. Combing over the past and prospecting about the future are certainly traits common to the human race – but equally, so is invention and fantasy. You only have to look at the dreams we have while sleeping for evidence of just how far beyond the realms of reality our mind can take us. Whether it be flying through the air or fighting a monster, our subconscious is rarely concerned by what is literally possible.

Most of the time, this is all well and good. In fact, as clearly outlined by this book itself, it can even be wonderful and positive. But what happens when those same daydreams become extensively elaborate, or excessively vivid? What about if they start to take up more of your time, until the life inside your head seems richer than the one out there in the real world? Well, needless to say, then we have hit something of a problem.

In a short story entitled 'The Secret Life of Walter Mitty' published in the *New Yorker* in 1939, author James Thurber fictionalized his own tendency to daydream by writing about a quiet, shy man who often retreats into his imagination where he cooks up dreams of heroism and victory (Thurber, 1939). In the time since, 'Walter Mitty' has become a shorthand term for a person who is ditsy and passive – a way of characterizing an individual who spends their time with their head in the clouds rather than out there in the real world. There's even been a film adaptation of the text, with Walter played by actor Ben Stiller – in this version of the story, Walter must learn the value of participating in the real world by starting to act, rather than just dream.

For the purposes of this chapter, Walter Mitty provides a perfect example of a genuine cognitive condition known as maladaptive daydreaming. This is a type of mind wandering that presents in an unhealthy way and can even bring with it adverse side effects. The line between maladaptive daydreaming and regular daydreaming can sometimes be a shaky one. Certainly James Thurber's own tendency to daydream provided him with rich fodder for a story and character that has stood the test of time – and yet, if he'd spent all of his time in his own head, he'd likely never have got around to writing it at all.

Before we go any further, we need to better understand what maladaptive daydreaming actually is. Let's take a look at a definition from the Maladaptive Daydreaming Centre.

WHAT IS MALADAPTIVE DAYDREAMING?

Maladaptive daydreaming occurs when a person engages in prolonged bouts of daydreaming, often for hours at a time, to cope with a problem. The daydreaming is 'maladaptive' because it causes significant distress and impairment. The daydreams are often vivid and complex plots that elicit a great deal of emotion. A person becomes so consumed by their daydream they may fail to complete work and other daily tasks, or start to withdraw from friends and family. (Fisher, 2024)

THE MALADAPTIVE DAYDREAMING SYMPTOM LIST

- Intensely vivid daydreams featuring distinct characters, settings, plots and intricate story elements, indicative of a rich inner world.

- Maladaptive daydreams are often sparked by real-life events (something in real life will act as a prompt to send the daydreamer into their own mind).

- Struggles in completing routine tasks due to preoccupation with daydreaming.

- Difficulty falling asleep at night, potentially linked to the immersive nature of daydreams.

- Persistent and overwhelming urge to prolong daydreaming sessions, even at the cost of other responsibilities.

- Engagement in repetitive movements and facial expressions during daydreaming episodes.

- Whispering and talking aloud while immersed in daydreams.

- Extended periods of daydreaming, lasting several hours.

- Significant emotional distress related to the frequency and intensity of daydreaming.

- Recognition that the internal fantasy world differs substantially from external reality resulting in shame and/ or guilt.

Symptom information taken from Healthline (Cirino, 2017).

Of course, you don't have to be a chronic or perpetual maladaptive daydreamer to have suffered bouts of mal-adaptive daydreaming (MD) in your life thus far. The term was first defined by Eli Somer, but has since gained consid-erable traction and interest from a broader audience (Somer, 2002). While it might be easy to laugh off the side effects of spending a little too much time daydreaming, for many people this is a real and worrying issue – which is why it's crucially important that making time for focused daydreaming doesn't become a gateway to this unhealthier habit. Being able to recognize MD is key to avoiding it – so we can ensure that the type of mind wandering we're engaging in is truly beneficial to our wellbeing and mental state.

A survey conducted online among individuals experi-encing MD revealed that 82 per cent experienced feelings of shame, while only 23 per cent had sought professional assistance for the issue (Bigelsen and Schupak, 2011). In most instances, it seems that MD comes about as a con-sequence of other mental health conditions or difficult personal circumstances. The instinct to retreat into fantasy is ultimately a coping mechanism – a way of escaping from the present into the comfort and safety of a world entirely within your control. Luckily, there are some clear and notable differences between the kind of mind wandering that is helpful for our brains and the pitfalls of MD.

While focused daydreaming should certainly be enjoy-able, it should not become so immersive that you feel totally detached from yourself and your surroundings. It is one of the characteristics of MD that the daydreamer actually dissociates from the world around them – this can then lead to knock-on effects in terms of relationships, performance at work and even in quality and duration of sleep. The Sleep Foundation notes that 'daydreams are a normal part of existence [...] while they distract us from the task at hand, they have several benefits such as the ability to plan future events, relieve ourselves from boredom, find meaning in our life's story, and boost our creativity' (Summer, 2021).

One study also further distinguished MD from typical daydreaming, finding that a positive and constructive form of daydreaming was correlated with curiosity and openness to experience. This is clearly at odds with MD, which causes an individual to retreat into themselves and avoid the experiences on offer in the world around them. The same study also identified two other maladaptive styles of daydreaming: guilty-dysphoric (connected with neuroticism) and poor attentional control (associated with lower levels of conscientiousness) (Somer et al, 2016). The latter is especially rife in our burned-out work culture, with our attention spans fractured from overstimulation and device use, which is why we must be extra cautious to not allow focused daydreaming to become another chip in our focus.

Being aware of the possibility of slipping into MD is the first step to avoiding it. This doesn't mean you can't enjoy fantastical mind-wandering sessions, or that there should never be some element of escapism to your daydreaming, but instead that these periods should not be excessive or last a prolonged period of time. It's also why a strategic approach is really key to applying focused daydreaming in a meaningful way.

Simply put, the ad-hoc application of the focused daydreaming technique will only reap ad-hoc results. If what you're seeking is real neurological benefits that help to prevent burnout and boost mental clarity, then you need to be able to approach the technique with the earnestness you would any other method for self-improvement.

It's important to say, also, that MD is not something to be overly afraid of. In fact, there's good reason to believe that mind wandering in an intentional manner might act as a natural antidote to MD as it promotes productivity and active engagement in the world around you. Still, knowing what to avoid – and equally what to embrace – can be incredibly beneficial to seeing real change.

Daydream-backed memories

In contrast to MD, focused daydreaming actually better equips us to deal with the world around us. It does this in a number of ways, but most crucially by restoring our cognitive capacities so we are operating at our best when tackling the grit and gristle of day-to-day work. What's more, daydreaming can even help to preserve the quality of what we already know. Memory can be a slippery thing, and with our attention always divided, holding onto information can be trickier still.

It seems contradictory, in a way, that spending time paying less attention would enable us to solidify and resurface the memories we do have – and yet this seems to be the case. It's important to remember, of course, that daydreaming is in fact something we're doing all the time. Researcher Anna Chambers at the Institute of Basic Medical Sciences at the University of Ohio told

Neuroscience News: 'We daydream for brief moments thousands of times a day, often just for a few seconds at a time' (Neuroscience News, 2022). But what is actually happening in those moments when it comes to our brain's activity, and what does this role play in forming and retaining memory?

Chambers sought an answer when she looked into how long-term memories are stored neurologically. Inside our brains, there is a three-centimetre-long sausage-shaped region called the hippocampus. This region of the brain receives a lot of information and impressions and is perhaps most important in creating memories. However, after a certain amount of time, the memories move on.

This is something Professor Koen Vervaeke elaborates on, too, explaining to *Neuroscience News* that we are usually less aware of what is happening around us when we are in a state of 'quiet wakefulness', and therefore our minds begin to daydream and wander. He says that when we are in this state, the hippocampus sends electrical impulses that encode various memories. He compares this to how different barcodes uniquely identify a product at a store. This happens thousands of times a day without us even being aware of it – even when we think we are not doing anything useful, our brains are actually very busy storing new memories (Neuroscience News, 2022).

This research is backed up by a study undertaken by scientists in Norway who used optogenetics to investigate brain activity in mice during periods of 'quiet wakefulness' that mirror mind wandering in humans (Bergland, 2022). During this vivo mouse study, they found that specific cells in the thalamocortical circuits that send sensory signals from the body to the cortex via the thalamus are briefly silenced for a few seconds before the hippocampus emits faint flow-wave ripples (sharp wave ripple or SWR) of memory.

Put in plainer language, it seems that faint whispers of memory are sent from the hippocampus in slow-wave ripples to the cortex. The momentary silence in the brain thus makes it easier for the cortex to 'hear' these SWR-related signals (Bergland, 2022). This is why daydreaming is good for forming new memories and re-engaging with older memories. While it's easy to underestimate the role memory plays in our life, it is actually an incredibly important feature of our cognitive make up – and indeed something that has an influence even on your very sense of self.

Think of it this way: without your memory, you wouldn't have any sense of a continuous identity. It is our memory which supplements our own idea of selfhood and provides a story and arc to our life as it has unfolded thus far. Plus, our memories also provide us with information.

As clearly evidenced already, the below-conscious levels of our mind work in abstract and elusive ways. Our subconscious might blend and intersperse seemingly irrelevant experiences and fragments of information to produce novel ideas in answer to a pressing situation you are facing right now. Who knows where it might draw this creativity from? There's no reason it might not take some recent learning and mix it with a skill or perspective you encountered over a decade ago. Don't forget: this part of the mind does not think in the same, linear way we do in our conscious brain – and this is exactly what gives it such broad creative potential.

Of course, all this is not to mention that our personal memory is also one of the truly unique things about us. While we certainly can and do enjoy the beauty of our shared memories, there is not a single person (alive or dead) who has had the exact same experiences as you. This is one of the wonderful things about being human, and is also why every single person genuinely has a valuable perspective to offer, even if they think themselves non-creative or unimportant.

No matter where your life has taken you, both the good and bad times provide rich and distinct inspiration for new, creative ideas and insights. You might think of our memory as many threads of different colours – when we allow our mind to wander more often, we give our brain more time to embroider those shades into a rich tapestry which both gives us a sense of history and aids us in the creation of new ideas and perspectives.

Given this, it's hardly surprising, then, that research links a high-quality memory to an increased sense of purpose. It actually seems that these two things can supplement each other, with a more vivid recall in turn solidifying a generalized feeling of purpose and direction in life. While we may daydream many times a day without meaning to, learning to apply this technique strategically and routinely gives our brains the chance to more regularly encode and access memories. (Science Daily, 2023).

Clearly, improved memory is just another one of the many benefits of focused daydreaming – but it's also something that we have begun to underestimate of late. It seems as we live through an age of distraction, we have idolized more and more the present moment. Doubtless, this is not a bad thing – but as with all things in life, it is balance between the two that is really key. By choosing to dip out of the present moment here and there, we reinforce our retention of the times we were awake and aware of the world around us.

Mindfulness or mindlessness?

Meditation and mindfulness are hot topics. These techniques – both of which are derived from ancient Eastern traditions – have gained traction at lightning speed as ways to improve wellbeing, and even to help boost focus. Today, you will find a multitude of apps and an endless stream of videos instructing you on how to clear your mind and tune into the present moment.

Oftentimes, the terms meditation and mindfulness get used interchangeably, and while they are related, they do actually have distinct definitions. As a broad term, 'meditation' may refer to a number of methods for focusing your attention or awareness – usually this is done by applying a particular technique (such as counting breaths or humming). In most cases, mindfulness is the desired outcome or end goal of meditation. Mindfulness refers to a state in which a person is able to keep their awareness fixed on the present moment – in other words, a way to avoid getting caught in the tumble of thoughts and anxieties we all experience at times. We are being mindful when we stay alive to what is literally happening in the world around us.

Both meditation and mindfulness have many associated benefits. In particular, mindfulness is frequently touted as a natural antidote to MD – and it's not hard to see why. If MD is characterized by a tendency to become overly absorbed by your thoughts, then mindfulness is a natural salve to this. There's no doubt that meditation and mindfulness are helpful tools for a number of people. A wealth of research shows that they can boost a person's mood, improve their focus and generally offer a whole host of wellbeing benefits (Davis and Hayes, 2012). Even so, it's important that we also distinguish these tools from focused daydreaming.

Sometimes in conversations about the power of daydreaming, I encounter confusion around the distinction between mindfulness and mind wandering. It's not entirely hard to understand why. In fact, a 'full' mind is in many ways an apt description of what it feels like to be in the thick of a daydreaming session – as different thoughts and ideas flicker through our mind, it certainly feels as if our head is full (and hence mindful). Yet, mindfulness and daydreaming are actually notably different. Especially as, if done correctly, a mindful person should actually be experiencing a dearth of thoughts.

If I asked you to practise a moment of mindfulness now you would undoubtedly be able to do it. Even just taking a slow breath in and out, paying attention to both the inhale and exhale, counts as being mindful. However, if I were to ask you to continue to be mindful for several minutes without break, it would quickly become more challenging. Wandering thoughts – as we've already outlined – are a natural feature of the human brain. While you might be able to hold your attention on your breath for a few moments, after a minute or two you'd soon find thoughts occurring all on their own.

This is exactly why meditation exists in the first place. It brings technique and discipline to the act of achieving mindfulness so that you can improve and enhance your ability to exist in the present moment. In many ways, the act of refocusing your mind is the most important aspect of meditation (like doing reps at the gym, it is when we engage the muscle that we're actually building strength).

It may sound obvious upon examination, but mind wandering is vastly different to this. Instead of trying to hold our mind still, it requires that we throw off the constraints of concentration and let our thoughts roam where they may. At least to an extent. Focused daydreaming does require that you bring a little more awareness to the process, avoiding those negative forms of mind wandering such as worrying or overthinking. And, as we've just looked at, being wary of the potential to become too immersed in your daydreams and getting wrapped up in MD.

Of course, this isn't to say the two techniques can't be complementary to each other, or that you must pick one tack or another. Indeed, mindfulness can even be an effective way of absorbing the world around you with more attentiveness in order to provide your subconscious with more creative fuel.

Still, I feel that one of the beauties of focused mind wandering is that most people find it a more accessible technique – and it still comes with a large number of cognitive benefits. In our overwhelming modern work environment, turning our thoughts off altogether can feel borderline impossible. By contrast, mind wandering is something we're all able to do. The momentum of our thoughts, and their content, is for many people a more effective way of giving the focused mind some respite.

Summary: daydreaming the right way

In this chapter, we looked at the importance of taking focused daydreaming seriously, drawing parallels between the commitment needed for focused daydreaming and other more 'conventional' goals. After all, this isn't a technique we can apply in a frivolous way if we want real results. Indeed, there are some forms of mind wandering that are not beneficial.

One of these less 'positive' forms of daydreaming is known as maladaptive daydreaming (MD), a type of compulsive daydreaming that can lead to adverse effects. The distinction between regular daydreaming and maladaptive daydreaming can be most clearly seen in terms of outcome – while regular daydreaming leaves you feeling positive and more open to experience, MD is excessive and often causes the dreamer to withdraw more and more into their own internal world.

We also looked at the benefits of focused daydreaming and its role in memory consolidation. This is why, when done correctly, focused daydreaming has the scope to actually improve our sense of self and the way in which we think and operate in the world.

We also considered different cognitive techniques that might be considered similar to daydreaming, but actually work in quite different ways – specifically, meditation and mindfulness. While these two tools work (often in tandem) to offer peace of mind and focus, daydreaming provides a more playful and organic path to achieving similar results. Overall, strategy and personal discernment are crucial in applying focused daydreaming, which brings real benefits and big picture thinking.

CHAPTER EIGHT

Harness the power of focused daydreaming

Well, by now, I hope we're in agreement: the state of the modern workplace is far from desirable. Busy Fool Syndrome (BFS) has become the dominant mode of working – and the cost to our focus, mental resilience and creative capacity has been hefty. I would also hope that with the evidence presented thus far you feel, like me, that daydreaming is the best-kept secret for rejuvenated cognitive function. But what about that intentional part, and how to actually make focused daydreaming a part of your daily routine?

I'll be honest: as simple and easy as this method is to apply, it will still require real dedication and commitment from you if you want to reap consistent results. The good news, however, is that the scope for success – when applied correctly – is unlimited.

Becoming a focused daydreamer will leave you feeling better rested and more motivated, all whilst helping you deliver work that reflects your fullest potential. While you're riding high on this dose of positivity, though, let me also warn you that to apply focused daydreaming means to swim against the tide of what is expected of the modern worker. Blazing your own path is frequently a characteristic of successful people, but that does not mean it is always easy. Humans are communal animals, and sometimes those who stray beyond convention are regarded with suspicion. But let me assure you that the rewards of doing so are worth any initial discomfort (and your results might just help you win over others, to boot).

Of course, in an ideal world, everyone would be on board with focused daydreaming – both in terms of using this tool themselves and in supporting others who use it. After all, the benefits are undeniable. Unfortunately, even on a cultural level, many have developed what could best be described as a co-dependent relationship with BFS. As covered in previous chapters, this can often be a self-sustaining system. When we become so ingrained and entrenched in a particular way of working, we eventually fail to notice that we are still employing a particular working structure (even if that structure is a toxic one) as it quickly becomes so ubiquitous as to be ultimately invisible.

Many have learned to measure not just their productivity by the amount of hours they have worked, but their very self-worth. Indeed, this might even be something you suffer from yourself. This makes the process of disentangling from this unhealthy working system even more complex as making time for focused daydreaming breaks can initially trigger guilt and even shame. Never underestimate the destructive power of such emotions, but also know that they can certainly be overcome.

As so often is the case, awareness is the first step to being able to avoid the pitfalls of these negative feelings so that you can tap into better emotional regulation and stability. Self-compassion is also a key ingredient here. It can be easy to shrug off the power of being kind to yourself, but given that negative self-talk can trigger anxiety and procrastination, it always pays to extend yourself some gentleness.

I'm always keen to remind people that being kind to yourself does not mean that you are lazy, or indeed that you can avoid accountability. Instead, it's about reminding yourself that you're doing the best you can with where you are, and that every moment is a fresh new moment full of renewed potential. This state of mind is much more likely to motivate actual change and action than the rankling gnawing of the self-critical mind.

So, all this is to say that, if you ever find yourself suffering from the nag of guilt while on a daydreaming break, pause for a moment and remind yourself of the facts. The time you spend away from focused work is not lazy and unproductive; on the contrary, it gives your brain more scope to be better focused and more creative on both the small and big scale. When in doubt, return to the story of the slowly boiled frog. Furiously treading water isn't going to do anything to stop the temperature rising, but hopping out of the water really will save your skin.

Naturally, all the reasons just discussed – the difficulty in going against the dominant working system and the process of unlearning the associated guilt and shame – are also the precise reasons that structure is key. You'll have heard it in countless other contexts before, but (like it or not) it is true that results don't happen overnight. And yet, I can at least assure you that with focused daydreaming you might just begin to experience the benefits more quickly than you might expect.

We've already touched on the metaphor of health and fitness, but it really is relevant here. For some reason, on a societal level, we rarely give the same consideration to our neurological health as we do our physical body. But really, so much of the same general logic applies to the brain too. If you don't exercise regularly or eat a balanced diet, it will naturally feel daunting and challenging if you then sign yourself up to run a marathon. In many ways, this is what we're doing every day in our current work culture: treating our brains poorly and then acting surprised when we burn out or struggle when faced with a big project.

Putting focused daydreaming into practice is like going to the gym. Weaving it into your routine at opportune moments is like eating healthily. Doing both these things on a regular basis is much the same as implementing a robust nutrition and fitness plan in unison. That is why focused daydreamers are in such fine cognitive condition – able to not only apply more focus and creativity in their work, but also to be more resilient to challenges and distractions when they do crop up.

So, how to achieve this? In this chapter, we'll look at different techniques to get you into the ideal daydreaming state, how you can make this a bespoke part of your routine, and how to monitor and track your own results. So, without further ado, here's how to create your very own DIY focused daydream toolkit!

Where do you like to wander?

On the surface, daydreaming should be easy, right? After all, I've just spent quite a considerable chunk of pages telling you how often you do it – even without meaning to – and how naturally it occurs as a part of normal cognitive functioning. The spanner in the works, of course, is that we've disrupted our natural tendency for mind wandering through our workplace inclination for BFS. What's more, through the constant presence of our devices and our reliance on entertainment for continuous neurostimulation, we have inadvertently impaired our ability to get into the position in which daydreaming naturally occurs.

But worry not! This is exactly what focused daydreaming is about. In order to be intentional with our daydreaming practice, we need to be able to enter the daydreaming state with efficiency and effectiveness. What's more, we want to be able to ensure that when we are in the mind-wandering state, it is in a manner that will be both restorative and fruitful. As already laid out, this means sidestepping a tendency to worry by ensuring our thoughts are free-moving and positive. Equally, it also means being wary of becoming overly involved in our daydreams in such a way that might lead to maladaptive daydreaming.

I should disclaim upfront that there is no single form of daydreaming that will be most beneficial to every single person. Just as we might agree that a walk in the fresh air is good for the vast majority of people, that doesn't mean we'll all have the same preference on where we take that walk – some people might prefer a wander through a wood or forest, others a meadow, and some a beach or mountain.

You likely already have an idea of the situations in which your mind is most prone to wander as it is, and the associated quality of daydreams that come in these different contexts. Still, even if you don't, simply knowing to pay more attention from here on in will help you connect with what works for you. In all likelihood, you're probably already aware on some level of the kinds of activities that bring you mental clarity. For example, have you always found a good walk clears your head? Or maybe you notice your thoughts tend to drift in a pleasant way when left beside an open window?

All this isn't to say that there's only one type of daydreaming that will work best as a prompt for you, but merely that it's worth noting the kinds of situations that do organically encourage this kind of free thinking and mind wandering.

Remember: the more connective and wide-ranging your thoughts, the better. So, when you find yourself in this state of mind, take a moment to notice what might have triggered it and look for ways to weave this into your own daydreaming schedule.

Directing the daydream

And action! The content and direction of our daydreams are sometimes ephemeral and seemingly random. In some ways, we have an influence over what we daydream about, and yet often these thoughts will naturally begin to spin away from our original starting point and head in a new direction of their own accord. But does what you daydream about really matter, especially when practising focused daydreaming? Well, the short answer is: yes, sort of.

Researchers have found that the kind of daydreaming we engage in does have an impact on the outcomes we then experience as a result. Positive and constructive forms of daydreaming are associated with higher creativity, while having difficulty focusing attention (poor attentional control) is linked to lower creativity. So, it is not just the content of our daydreams that has an effect, but the state of mind and structure we bring to a mind-wandering session.

In undertaking this particular study, researchers made use of a machine learning approach to analyse brain activity and see how it related to different types of daydreaming. Through this, they found that these different types of brain patterns could actually successfully predict an individual's level of creativity.

The brain regions involved in daydreaming and creativity are – as we know – part of the neurological networks responsible for self-reflection, decision-making, and attention. This particular study found that positive forms of daydreaming were associated with planning, as well as vivid and pleasant thoughts, and were most often fuelled by curiosity. These traits also left daydreamers more open to experiences – something which solidified the link between this form of mind wandering to creative thinking and imaginative ideas.

By contrast, the more harmful forms of daydreaming were associated with poor attentional control and were correlated with the inability to focus – not only externally, but internally. Perhaps inevitably, this unhelpful form of mind wandering is negatively associated with creative ability. While taking time away from a task to spend some time daydreaming in a constructive manner might enable us to boost our creative thought, if we're not able to concentrate when the time comes to actually produce work, then our good ideas – if they are there – naturally go to waste. This is to say, when our attention is scattered or inconsistent, it can hinder the cognitive processes involved in creative thinking (Sun et al, 2021).

So, in other words, the content of our daydreams can also have an effect on the quality of our cognitive output. Naturally, you don't want to exert too much control over your daydreams when taking regular mind-wandering breaks – part of the respite experienced during this time comes from the freedom of letting your thoughts roam where they may. But that doesn't mean you can't encourage the most creativity-aligned thoughts by leaning into the ideas that most naturally spark your curiosity and seem to be especially vivid. In other words, you can let your mind lead the way – just give it a nudge here and there to keep it heading in a sunny direction.

Three steps to success

Before we look more at what activities might actually be helpful for allowing you to access the mind-wandering state, we need to remind ourselves of the three key steps that make up the focused daydreaming technique. Though we've already outlined these steps at a basic level in previous chapters, now feels like a good time to look at them with more scrutiny and in greater detail.

Of course, on the most basic level these three key steps are easy to understand and simple to apply. Still, I think it's important that we understand the methodology that sits behind them. This way, we can better apply that logic in our own lives – understanding exactly why each step is necessary.

Step 1: Find your focus

It wouldn't be focused daydreaming if you didn't also have a specific intention in mind. When focused daydreaming (ideally) becomes a daily habit for you, it may initially seem something of a chore to always begin a mind-wandering session by setting an intention – but doing so is an important part of the process. Here's why.

Intention is about more than just direction or focus. Intention involves the alignment of our actions with our values, ambitions and beliefs. It also refers to the real root of what motivates us. We might think of it this way: you might be focused on doing a good job, but the reasons for that relate most closely to your intent – those intentions might be numerous or intersecting. Perhaps they relate to your desire to be successful in your job, or connect with your teammates at work, or even simply a hunger for progress and new experiences.

Whatever the case, we can see clearly how intent is, arguably, even more powerful and nuanced than just your bog-standard goal setting. It reflects, on the most honest level, what you hope to achieve by taking a certain action. This is exactly why I have opted to use this word as a prefix to the kind of daydreaming I am recommending in this book. That's not to mention that intention also brings a level of awareness and action into the overall process. In my mind, the whole point of focused daydreaming is that it helps to remove the randomness of the creative process – and demystifies the way to make regular focus an easy and repeatable process.

Interestingly, intentions, according to Buddhist philosophy, play a crucial role in the concept of karma, influencing our future based on the energy created by our actions and their underlying intentions. According to this philosophy, by checking beliefs and clarifying intentions we can align our actions with our intentions, leading to a more confident, vibrant and meaningful life (Scotti, 2023).

While you certainly don't need to worry about karma or ancient philosophy when setting your intention for your daydreaming sessions, that idea of checking beliefs and clarifying your desired goal for that particular session can certainly be beneficial. Setting an intention doesn't need to require an extreme amount of forethought, or even elaborate planning. On some occasions it may be as simple as acknowledging to yourself what your ultimate intention is before starting that daydream session.

Still, I do find that – where possible – making space for just briefly noting down, each day, exactly what your intention is can be helpful. This is for two reasons: one is that, over time, it will help you get better at actually setting these intentions. As you do this more regularly, it will become easier to identify the core idea that is driving you forward. That means being able to peel away the outer layers of any goal and find the root of what's important so that your subconscious can really hone in on that focus.

The second reason is that by keeping a record of your intention you can also more actively keep track of when it comes to fruition. You might even want to tick these intentions off as you uncover ideas and resolutions that have helped you fulfil the intentions you originally outlined! Doing so will certainly strengthen your belief in the power of focused daydreaming, and ultimately help to keep you consistent in making daydreaming a daily habit.

Of course, you might wonder what some intentions for a daydreaming session might actually look like – check out below to get an idea of the kinds of intentions you can set, along with some analysis on the why behind it.

EXAMPLES OF INTENTIONS AND RELATED ANALYSIS

Intention: 'My intention is to better understand the problem currently stumping my team.'

Analysis: This intention is clear and simple. You'll notice it doesn't, at this point, even mention resolving the problem that is causing the issue. As focused daydreaming is something you do regularly, you don't need to overburden the intention of a single session with an overly ambitious goal.

Mind wandering brings clarity and insight, as well as solutions and creativity. An intention like this is a great starting point for enabling you to better engage and get to grips with a problem you're struggling with – especially if it's an intention you set alongside other members of your team, making time to regroup and report any new understandings you've reached.

Of course, as time goes on you can build on this intention to actually focus on solutions too. Indeed, sometimes they may pop up anyway!

Intention: 'My intention is to reimagine how I might reorganize my average day in order to be more efficient and retain mental clarity.'

Analysis: This is an interesting intention, because people tend to think of the daydreaming tool as something that is solely for work – in the sense of tasks, projects and ideas. But you do not need to limit yourself in this way. Focused daydreaming can also be used in more lateral ways to improve your overall approach to life.

If you're feeling uninspired day-to-day, or like your working system needs a jolt, there's no reason you can't also make this a part of your intention when engaging in a daydream break. The trouble with creating a new working routine is that, by its nature, routine is something we're so used to that we no longer see it with objectivity.

That's why setting an intention to shake it up can be powerful – giving your subconscious something to chew on so it can ultimately disrupt your current way of working and throw up new ideas on how you might reimagine your current working systems. Really, this same intention or technique can be adapted and applied in a variety of forms. Whether it's wanting to be able to think of ways to bring more energy to your day, or finding a new perspective on daily problems, focused daydreaming can be a route to a whole new way of living life.

Intention: 'My intention is to feel more energetic and creatively refuelled.'

Analysis: This intention is a good example of how goal setting in this way doesn't always have to be niche or specific. Of course, it can be – and on many occasions this might be helpful. Still, we all have down periods in work when our tasks are ticking over and there's nothing pressing to demand our attention. In such moments, finding energy and motivation is often our biggest challenge. This is especially true if we're lacking pressing deadlines or exciting new projects to motivate us.

Well, needless to say, such a moment is perfect for an intention like this. It tells your subconscious to look at the raw materials you're working with day-to-day, and get to work with creative new ways you might engage with this content. Even with the most mundane or niggly work, a change in mindset and energy can render what once seemed tiresome, suddenly new and exciting. So, on the days when you're not sure what you want, a broader intention like this can act as a simple and effective way to inject a bit of life and purpose back into what you're doing.

Step 2: Information for inspiration

What's a canvas without some paint? You know by now the role of the subconscious in the creative process. When we switch off and tune out, our default mode network lights up, our subconscious comes online, and while we're busying ourselves with a variety of daydreams, our mind is hard at work making connections and forming fresh ideas.

We might think of our subconscious as a workshop. It will remain in operation even if we don't supply it with particular tools, but if we want a specific end product, we probably want to make sure the right materials are supplied. After all, if you need a wooden armchair, you don't want to hand over a scrapheap of metal. And so, this is where information for inspiration comes in and – needless to say – the information you input should relate to the intention you've already set.

For example, if you know your intention for your next daydream break is to come up with ideas for a meeting about driving marketing engagement, you can put some time aside to familiarize yourself with this topic. The great thing about this stage is you can let yourself off the hook in terms of being actively creative in the moment (something that is often stifling anyway, the pressure to generate ideas causing you to feel limited). Instead, your sole purpose is to gather all the raw materials your mind might need to get creatively busy with it.

The idea of sourcing information for inspiration can seem daunting at first but I'm here to tell you there's no reason to be intimidated. There are so many different ways of uncovering material that might later influence and supply the ideas you cook up – both in obvious places and more obscure ones. While, by the nature of this method and its flexibility, there is no cookie-cutter way to find this information, I can provide some suggestions of intentions and ways you might go about finding inspiration to fulfil your goal. Please note, however, that the below is not prescriptive – there are really endless ways you might go about sourcing inspiration.

FINDING INSPIRATION

Intention: 'Come up with innovative ways to attract new customers.'

Inspiration: Here, you might fuel up your subconscious by looking at case studies of successful marketing campaigns – within your own industry but also outside it. You could also spend some time reacquainting yourself with your most successful routes for customer acquisition at present, as well as the areas in which you are not performing as well. You could comb through feedback from existing customers, or even spend some time designing a survey to get more intel.

I like to think of the intention of my mind-wandering session as the heart of my action – with all the ideas that spring off from this centre as potential areas of interest. That's all to say, follow your nose. Get to know the topic you're working on better and from multiple angles, you might just be able to bring together ideas from unexpected places to hit on a novel selling point for bringing in new customers.

Intention: 'Feel more confident putting forward ideas in meetings.'

Inspiration: An intention like this might seem harder to wise up on as it is broader, but there's still plenty you can do to fill your subconscious with material that it can then turn into inspiration for fulfilling such a goal. The way I see it, there are three aspects to this particular intention – one is the hope to be more confident, another is to have more ideas, and the final part is the combination of the two, i.e. having the confidence in your own ideas to feel capable of putting them forward.

Well, moving on from that three-pronged approach, you might spend some time consuming information about how you can build your confidence. This might be in any form, but ideally one that speaks and resonates with you – whether that's a podcast, a TED talk or an article. From here, you might spend some time diving into other general areas you find interesting – of course, that could be related to the topics you're hoping to discuss in work meetings, but even areas of general curiosity are good for getting creative momentum spinning in your subconscious.

With an intention like this, you can also spend some time actively daydreaming about the outcome. In other words, visualizing how it might look and feel to be able to present your ideas with confidence in the meeting. In such a moment, you are still allowing your mind to enter the daydream state, but also providing the added oomph of positive visualization, a technique that is even applied by Olympic athletes in order to help improve their performance when competing.

Intention: 'Find new ways to do routine tasks.'
Inspiration: Isn't this something we could all do with getting a little better at? We all have tasks we must work through every day. Sometimes these kinds of tasks are not enjoyable, but they are necessary. Finding new ways to

approach work like this can often make a huge difference to the quality of your days and overall work – but finding the energy and inspiration to do that is a challenge when there are a million and one other things to contend with.

You may also wonder, with an intention like this, how exactly you go about consuming information that might give your subconscious something to work with as there's not necessarily an obvious way to gather information about your own specific routine tasks. Well, at least ostensibly. That's why this intention is an interesting one to explore here, as the process of looking for inspiration actually can simply mean diving into your own processes.

In this case, that might mean timing how long certain tasks take you, and maybe taking note of what you do and don't enjoy about these tasks – equally, you might track the qualities of the work you do enjoy. On the surface, this may sound a strange or even fruitless way of improving processes, but in tandem with your set intention and ultimate daydreaming session, you may just be surprised. The focused daydreaming technique is truly incredible when it comes to shining a light on dynamic new ways of working.

Step 3: Activate the daydream state

So, we arrive at the third and final step – and undoubtedly the most important of them all. That is, actually getting into the daydreaming state. We've already covered the basics of the constructive mind-wandering state, but let's take a look again at the qualities associated with focused daydreaming done properly:

- **Free-moving and connective**. Focused daydreaming should not dawdle in one place but move freely through a whole range of topics – with one thought acting as a gateway to another.
- **Positive and pleasant**. Focused daydreaming makes you feel good; it does not involve dwelling on negative thoughts but is broadly positive and interesting, surfacing a range of topics and ideas – in other words, an adventure for the imagination!
- **Mind-broadening and confidence-building**. Focused daydreaming should not make you forget or dread returning back to the external world and present moment once over. Instead, it should increase your interest in life more broadly – stoking your curiosity and opening you up to new experiences and ideas.

So, how do we actually get into the state that facilitates this type of mind wandering? You'll be unsurprised to hear that there isn't one single route to success – and naturally, as already covered in this chapter, different things might work better for different people. It's important to say, as well, that these daydream breaks should not be without constraints. After all, your productivity isn't going to improve if you allow yourself to mind-wander the whole day away.

Ideally, I would recommend at least one focused daydreaming break of around half an hour taken once a day – but if that's challenging, there are other options. The most important thing is finding an amount of time you can commit to within your daily routine, every day, even if it is just for 10 minutes. Decide what is realistic for you, and from here on in make a commitment to fulfilling this period of focused daydreaming with regularity.

As I've touched upon before, haphazard application is a sure path to haphazard results. Equally, the benefits of committing are undeniable. This doesn't mean you can't trial different types of routine to find out what works for you – and indeed, one of the best things about focused daydreaming is that it can be fitted to suit both your way of thinking and your working routine. For some people, very brief mind-wandering breaks dispersed throughout the day might yield the best results. Others might prefer a single, longer daydreaming session each day. Whatever the case, make sure to take some time to stick with a single routine for at least a few weeks before moving on to another approach.

Now, to get to the important stuff – what should you actually be doing to get into the ideal daydreaming state? Certainly, if you feel capable of simply sitting and letting your mind wander, that can work well on occasion. However, I more often find that with the stress and over-whelm of the modern working world, it's preferable to have a prompt that can naturally prompt your mind to wander.

There are no hard and fast rules with this, but I always feel that the two good rules of thumb for picking a day-dreaming activity are monotonous or rhythmic. Tedious tasks such as chores are ideal because they often require a low level of concentration so that you can't do something else, but are boring enough that they still leave your mind free to wander. After all, many believe that relief from boredom is actually one of the functions of daydreaming in the first place – so as strange as it may sound, putting yourself in the position where you are bored may just be a good starting point for setting your thoughts wandering.

Similarly, rhythmic activities also act as an effective gateway to mind wandering. This can come in many forms: walking, running, doodling and even singing! These kinds of tasks can induce something akin to a trance-like state in which it is easier to allow our minds to drift and our imaginations to fire up.

While there is obviously a wide range of things that fit into these two categories, and there are certainly no limits on the activities you might use to find your best daydreaming mindset, the ideas below at least provide a few suggestions of activities you might try in your daily daydream breaks to find out what works best for you:

- **Something artsy.** While it might sound vague, arts and crafts can provide a great way for us to keep our hands busy and engage our imaginations while also leaving our minds free to wander. Still, I tend to prefer the word 'artsy' as it's important to note this isn't about creating a masterpiece – perfectionism is your enemy here.

  Instead, it's about making time for something that can give you a sense of creative purpose, while also prompting a natural daydream state. The activities that fall into this category are really endless: painting, drawing, doodling, stitching, knitting, pottery, embroidery – the options are limitless!

- **Exercise.** I know, I know. You hardly need another person telling you that exercising is good for both body and mind, but this recommendation does come with a caveat that for daydreaming purposes, there's no need to commit to vigorous or punishing exercise.

Instead, this is really about moving your body in a way that gets your thoughts moving. For many people, walking is more than effective enough to produce this effect – but for others, anything from dancing to swimming might induce this.

- **'What if?' scenarios.** Now, let's get this out the way upfront: by proposing you jump into some 'what if?' scenarios, this is not an excuse to fall into an anxious, worried state of mind. Instead, we're talking about stoking curiosity as a gateway to some fun frog-hopping thoughts, jumping from one idea to another. You could equally use 'why?' or 'and then what?' – start with a root idea and use such questions to encourage the tide of your thinking in new, interesting directions.

- **Get playful!** There is something inherently fun and playful about daydreaming. After all, you're in the realm of imagination and fantasy – this is not the time to bring buttoned-up, serious business energy. Instead, why not think of ways to be more playful day-to-day?

  There are so many ways you might do this, whether that's breaking out some nostalgic board games with your colleagues, climbing a tree, playing with Lego, or indulging in a childhood treat such as ice cream. Silly as it may sound, these kinds of activities are a great way to reconnect with the imaginative mindset of your childhood.

- **Chores or cleaning.** Yes, this next one might be in contrast to the last suggestion but it has equal potential to get your mind wandering – even if that's more likely to be out of boredom than a sense of fun. But even so, it's effective – plus, it is productive!

While this book clearly sets out a manifesto against multitasking, the one exception is allowing yourself to daydream while completing something more mundane – whether that be while doing the ironing, washing up, laundry or neatening up your desk.

- **Travel and commute time.** Most of us are in broad agreement about commuting: it's a necessary evil, but something most of us could really do without. Of course, these days with the rise of remote work, more and more people are more regularly cutting out this travel time.

  Well, whatever the case, commuting and travel actually provide us with a great chance to daydream – regardless of whether you're walking, driving or getting public transport, these all present an excellent opportunity to indulge the wandering mind. This in mind, maybe you can make more of the so-called 'dead' commute time after all.

- **Cooking.** If you're bored of the same old sandwiches for lunch every day, I might just have some good news for you. Cooking – or even just making food – is actually a great way to prompt some mind wandering.

  What's more, it can even provide some great mind-wandering material in itself. Taking time to plan or concoct your own recipe is actually a pretty good way to begin some daydreaming, and with any luck you'll be on to new topics without even realizing your thoughts have wandered to pastures new.

- **Make a mind map.** A mind map, (also known as a spider diagram or brainstorm), is actually an excellent visual representation of the wandering mind. With a central topic in the middle, and branches radiating out, each one with its own related or connected idea, it offers a symbolic stand-in for the way our mind naturally moves. Taking the time to mind-map out your thinking is a great way to do your daydreaming on the page when you're struggling to allow your mind to wander more organically. This is why we developed Ayoa.com, a cognitively sensible productivity and learning app, to use mind maps as the tool to start your work.

- **Embrace silence.** Yes, these days it can be a scary thing. But in our age of constant entertainment, a bit of silence can be precious indeed. Embracing silence doesn't have to mean dedicating yourself to a monastic life devoid of technology, but on occasions when you'd usually be tempted to put on a podcast or stream your favourite show, try instead to be in the moment and see what thoughts might naturally occur.

- **Listen to music.** Converse to the last suggestion, music can also actually be a great prompt for daydreaming. Why not make a playlist of music you find inspiring, moving or energizing? Then, on your daydream breaks, you can make this the soundtrack to your mind-wandering session – allow the songs to take you back into old memories or pave the way to new ideas and thoughts of the future.

- **Stop more often.** As clearly discussed, in our modern moment we are constantly go, go, go! Dynamism is so often our constant state, and this way of existing can be both overstimulating and addictive. It's no wonder, then, that when we are left with a free moment or idling time away, our first instinct is often to fill it with noise and action.

We do this in a variety of ways – whether that be reaching for our phone to scroll social media, or quickly arranging to do something in our free moment. Whatever the case, simply setting the intention to stop more often can be a great way to naturally encourage more frequent mind wandering. Even the five-minute break when you decided to sit rather than stare at your phone might over time sharpen your focus and help to uncover more creative ideas via the power of daydreaming.

Summary: daydreams for enhanced cogitation and innovation

Harnessing the power of focused daydreaming can significantly bolster focus, cognitive resilience and creative capacity by allowing you to helicopter out of your reactive mindset to see much more of the real landscape. However, making focused daydreaming a part of your routine demands commitment and dedication to reap the vast potential benefits. As with anything else that offers real impact, it must be treated with respect.

In this chapter, a wide range of techniques have been detailed to guide you into the optimal daydreaming state. These can be tailored to your daily routine to create a customizable and structured approach to focused daydreaming.

The transition towards a more beneficial work modality like focused daydreaming may initially induce feelings of guilt and shame due to deep-rooted work conventions. Overcoming these negative feelings is critical, and the first step toward achieving this is self-awareness. Empowering yourself through self-compassion and acknowledging your potential can effectively redeem negative self-image and drive positive change.

Focused daydreaming, like exercise, is conducive to cognitive health when regularly practised and integrated into daily routines. This method can not only enhance the focus and creativity of your work but also increase your resilience to challenges and distractions.

To implement focused daydreaming, you need to acquire a bespoke routine that includes being aware of where and how your mind tends to wander, directing the course of your daydreams and monitoring and tracking your results. The ability to slip into efficient and effective daydreaming states will ensure that your thoughts are both restorative and fruitful.

CHAPTER NINE

Escape Busy Fool Syndrome

So, we've made it this far. We now know just how toxic and pervasive Busy Fool Syndrome (BFS) is in the modern workplace. This unsustainable way of working benefits no one – least of all our brains. It's no wonder, in such an environment, that our focus has become flighty and divided.

With this context, we can at the very least extend ourselves more self-compassion for struggling to find creative energy in our day-to-day working lives. This is truly not an individual failing, but instead an inevitable outcome of the all-too-familiar set of circumstances impeding real, creative thinking in business, and indeed in our lives more broadly.

As we discussed at the very start of the book, our always-on, always-busy working culture has become the slowly boiling water which over time cooks the frog obliviously dwelling in the pot. At the top level, the framework set out thus far in this book should provide a clear solution – at least I hope it does. And yet, as so often is the case, the theory is one thing. Application is another beast altogether.

Still, let's recap the key facts of what we have covered so far in order to give context to how we might outline a template for real, meaningful implementation. In a world obsessed with busyness over productivity, our brains have become overstimulated, overwhelmed and – in many cases – actively burned out. The neurological cost of this constant stress is depleted focus, lethargy and a general sense of lacking purpose and creativity at work. It's a sad state of affairs that is not limited to one particular industry, or indeed any particular level of seniority or rank. In other words, this is a chronic condition.

As with all chronic conditions, rehabilitation takes time and effort. Treating the symptoms is not enough to really get on the path to lasting recovery; we need a holistic over-haul, a change in ethos and mindset as well as a technique to achieve just that. And so, enter focused daydreaming. The problem is, as a neurological tool, mind wandering has been continually overlooked and underestimated. But that can be changed.

Given the dismal context of overwhelm and burnout already outlined above, it'll come as a surprise to no one that daydreaming is viewed as little more than a frivolous bit of time-wasting. From the omnipresence of our devices to the endless options for communication via technology – in addition to a vast array of entertainment options – we no longer give our brains genuine idle time.

Constantly prodded and poked, our brains have, in response, become exhausted and numb. From this cognitive stupor has arisen a Catch-22 scenario in which our mental fatigue robs us of the imagination to work in more dynamic and ambitious ways, trapping us in a generalized pandemonium of busyness – which in turn feeds the burnout that keeps us too overwhelmed to do anything about it. As a scenario it may be far from ideal, but the good news is that there is a way out.

As a culture, we have forgotten – or at the very least overlooked – the important role daydreaming plays in our overall cognitive functioning. Far from an inconvenient flaw, a wealth of neuroscientific research proves that our brains are not inactive during periods of mind wandering. On the contrary, while we're lost in a stream of seemingly random thoughts and ideas, crucial cognitive regions of the brain (that is, those associated with memory, focus, creativity, problem solving and emotional wellbeing) come online. This is why great ideas so often strike us when we're doing something seemingly irrelevant – such as taking a bath or commuting to work. It's also why we return to work initially feeling more rested and resilient after a break or holiday.

Lest we dwell too long on what we've already covered (though a little repetition never hurts when it comes to enforcing our understanding and recall of an important topic) in order to find our focus, foster mental resilience and enjoy the many benefits of a creatively engaged mind, we need to start making time for daydreaming.

That is, not any old daydreaming, but what I have pitched to you as 'focused daydreaming'. By bringing focus into the daydreaming process (deciding ahead of time the outcome we'd like to achieve via a mind-wandering session) and the robustness of routine (making application a daily habit) we're able to not only foster mental resilience and offer our brain some much-needed respite, but newly direct and renew our general mental energy.

But here comes the tricky bit – making it stick. We all know how it goes. From New Year's Resolutions to health and fitness routines, it's easy to make plans for self-improvement but much harder to see them through to fruition. This is exactly why a change in mindset is non-negotiable for becoming a focused daydreamer. Of course, the most common response (or, more accurately, complaint) I hear when people discuss their concerns of putting this tool into practice is lack of time.

Listen, I understand. When our days and minds are both overflowing with a seemingly ceaseless number of tasks and responsibilities, making time for doing nothing – even when clued up on the benefits – is a hard thing to follow through on. That's why we need a vision for a new working world, and a strategy and tools that make applying focused daydreaming possible. After all, the world is changing. In this new working era, the positive creative traits nurtured by daydreaming will only become much more important.

Dreamers in a robotic world

Artificial Intelligence (AI) is changing the face of work – in fact, it's changing the face of society altogether. The AI advancements we've seen in the last few years are a part of the early stages of a whole new era. Just as the industrial revolution created many new jobs, and the internet changed the way we work in the office, AI will transform the workplace once more – and arguably even more dramatically than these previous two epochs.

Naturally, such change also comes with a great deal of anxiety. As AI becomes more competent and capable – performing increasingly complex roles – concern about humans being supplanted in the workplace altogether becomes more prominent, too. After all, what gives us the edge over machines when they're faster, more accurate and always available? Well, the answer is actually very simple – our creativity.

Anyone who has played around with the latest AI tools will know that, at least ostensibly, AI can be creative in the literal sense that it can generate new material. Indeed, it can even give off the illusion of creative prowess. Prompt one of these tools to write a poem or create a picture and it'll be able to do so in a matter of moments. What it won't be able to do, however, is offer real discernment on these things. An AI tool has no opinion on which of the ideas it produces are good. It can only mimic or imitate the creative work of humans. Without conscious experience to draw from, and so no inner life, AI cannot offer real evaluation of its ideas and how they might be used in a real-world context.

Lest we forget, at the most basic level, all AI tools are simply a sequence of complex algorithmic information. AI can certainly store an astounding amount of accurate data compared to the human brain, and it can learn to sequence and combine this information to produce helpful material and automate complex processes on request. However, this is not a replacement for genuine creative thinking – or indeed thinking more broadly. What's more, it means that the workplace of the future is one in which humans add value via their emotions, creativity and critical thinking abilities.

Consider for a moment all the annoying admin things you have to juggle every day. It might be anything from arranging meetings to sending emails. Think, also, about the time you spend on mundane or repetitive tasks – no matter your position, this is something we all have to handle from time to time. Now imagine that all these things were managed in their entirety by AI. How much extra time would you have? The answer is likely more considerable than you'd initially think, especially when you consider how often this kind of work punctuates the more important stuff – interrupting the flow of our more creative work. In this sense, it's clear that as AI becomes more ubiquitous in the workplace, one of the greatest resources it will provide us with is more time.

As we have covered previously, at its heart, creativity is just about the combining of different types of knowledge and material to form something new. In this sense, AI is speeding the whole process of creative generation up by giving us more material to work with, as well as new ways of organizing and presenting this information with increased efficiency. But that doesn't remove the need for humans altogether. The workplace of the future will be one in which humans and AI work in a hybrid manner in this sense, with more space for big creative ideas and more time for experimentation.

There's no denying it may take some time to reach this vision of the future, but what I am in effect describing is a workplace in which 'busy work' has been eradicated. After all, everything that would usually fall into the category of busy fool activities will soon be effectively managed by AI. This is exactly why those who are able to tap into their imagination, source creative ideas and generally keep a hold on sharpened mental clarity will flourish in this new era. Still, the road to reaching this point might be bumpy – and it is the early adopters of this new way of working who will reap the most success, on top of the other well-being benefits that come with this more enjoyable way of working.

Bringing the future forward is always a challenge. Humans are so often creatures of habit, and even when we have the tools and technology to advance, it is more often a stubborn mindset which holds us back from actually taking that next step forward.

A new way of working

Being a trailblazer is all well and good, but how do you tread a new path when caught in the crowd all marching the usual way? There is no single answer, of course, but when it comes to adopting focused daydreaming in your day-to-day work, there are a number of things you can do to make it a steadfast part of your routine.

The first thing is to make it a habit. In simple terms, habits are behaviours we perform regularly without the need for the emphasis of conscious thought or decision making. Naturally, these behaviours can be either beneficial to us or not, depending on what they are. You may have heard the phrase 'neurons that fire together, wire together' – what this actually refers to is how repeated behaviours, from a cognitive perspective, become easier to repeat.

So, how to make daydreaming a habit? Take a look at the following tips and suggestions.

Habitual mind wandering

Building new habits requires a deliberate and incremental approach. An intentional routine is the first step to achieving this as habits emerge as a result of our regular, repeated behaviours. When we try to apply a new activity in a haphazard way, we decrease our chances of imprinting this behaviour into our mind. In a similar vein, we're much more likely to give up if we over-commit to a huge change that disrupts or overturns our present routine. Conversely, adding a small commitment to your daily routine as it is at present provides the discipline and framework needed to transform a conscious behaviour into an ingrained habit.

Many people also praise the benefit of micro-habits. That is, small changes we can make that help us slowly integrate that change until – eventually – we achieve a bigger and complete shift in mindset. For focused daydreaming, this could be as simple as committing to just five minutes of mind wandering a day. Over time, when this becomes ingrained, you can begin to increase the amount of time you actually spend performing focused daydreaming to reap more benefits. But when in doubt, starting small is a good rule of thumb.

If you are worried about what it might look like to others in having 'focused daydreaming' appearing on your shared calendars at work, perhaps use other terms such as 'planning' or 'strategic thinking'. Just make sure you do allocate time, otherwise BFS may prevent loss of focus.

Start saying 'no'

This particular point sometimes elicits the occasional eye roll, and I get it. Anyone well acquainted with the business world will know that being told to say no more isn't exactly groundbreaking advice. People can sometimes be dismissive of advice that feels ubiquitous or overused, but in this instance, saying 'no' more is – like it or not – highly effective.

BFS is a condition actively exacerbated by agreeability. Of course, this might be hard to hear – after all, saying yes to colleagues and wanting to help others at work isn't in itself a bad trait, far from it. The problem is, we've reached a point where we feel increasingly obliged to others. If we see a message come through, or a request for a call or meeting, more often than not we'll just go along with it and hand over our time freely regardless of what else we have on.

There are a number of reasons for this, and principal among them is the working culture itself. When someone replies to your message promptly, for example, you feel obliged to do the same. Reciprocal behaviour is actually – from an evolutionary perspective – an important sociological trait that fosters societal cooperation. No wonder, then, that it can be hard to say no to colleagues. It's hardwired into us. And yet, this is exactly what you need to start doing if you want to quit being a busy fool and adopt focused daydreaming.

Really, saying no is actually about establishing better boundaries in order to protect your time. That means not just literally saying no to people but actually saying no to tasks that aren't pressing, in order to make time to focus on what really matters. One of the most crucial things here is chunking your communication. That means setting aside particular points in the day in which you'll reply to emails or messages, with a view to leaving the rest of your day free for real, productive work.

It can be challenging to begin with, but over time you'll begin to find that colleagues and team mates begin to respect and appreciate your new way of working. What's more, it's so often the case that people are more reasonable and understanding than we give them credit for. We feel – perhaps irrationally – that if we are honest in telling someone we don't have time for a particular piece of work they'll be annoyed, but this is not necessarily the case. At the end of the day there's only one way to find out.

Go undercover

Having said that people typically react better than you might expect to work boundaries, I do appreciate that this is not always the case. For a whole number of reasons, trying to quit Busy Fool Syndrome can be challenging. Often, setting time aside for focused daydreaming is one of the biggest barriers for people. Even when you are converted to the idea yourself, selling colleagues or senior team members on the productive benefits of doing nothing can be a daunting prospect. I'd always encourage openness and honesty where possible. Especially as such conversations can be an excellent point to implement a real cultural shift in business (and more on that next!).

However, when – for whatever the reason – this is too challenging, you can still go undercover to implement the core tenets of this working philosophy to your own advantage.

For this, I recommend micro-breaks. That is, miniature breaks for focused daydreaming that you can take at your desk if needed, without having to talk to anyone else about it. Of course, switching off and tuning out when still surrounded by your work can be more challenging, which is why I would usually recommend other daydreaming activities where possible. But when this isn't an option, you can still find ways to switch off and let your mind wander, whether that be by listening to some music, doing some doodling, or creating a mind map.

Cultural shift

There are workarounds for when the people you work with aren't on board with focused daydreaming – but they'll never be as beneficial as the alternative. And that is a real cultural change in the workplace. Of course, this will be easier to suggest and implement the more senior you are, but regardless of your level or role it could still be worth a conversation.

After all, you don't need to get the whole of your organisation on board immediately – it could be as simple as committing to regular focused daydreaming breaks as a team and tracking your collective success and sense of wellbeing. Really, the proof is in the pudding. Changing things at the level of company culture is no mean feat, but big changes start with small ones. Plus, by deciding to make focused daydreaming a serious part of your day in tandem with others, you also reap the added benefits of accountability.

Make mindset your priority

The truth is that none of this is likely to stick if you're not also embracing a positive mindset at the same time. I don't just mean this in a broad sense, but specifically related to focused daydreaming as a practice.

If you're feeling doubtful about the power of this technique to transform your life, you can always dip back into this book to remind yourself of the huge amount of research showing just how conclusive the link between mind wandering and enhanced cognitive function is. Don't forget, too, that even without the mind wandering, regular breaks are also linked to heightened productivity, focus and restored mental clarity.

The combination of the two really is so powerful, and applying this to your life in earnest is so much more than a small productivity hack. It has the potential to completely rewrite your day-to-day experience of work, and even your life beyond this. When woven religiously and seriously into your routine, it has the power to make you feel happier and energized, while also propelling you towards success with a firm grasp on the creative focus that has recently seemed elusive to so many of us.

Summary: forming the daydream habit

You now know about the state of the modern workplace. A culture of constant busyness hampers our focus and divides our attention. This chronic condition, prevalent across various industries and hierarchical levels, leads to burnout, depleted focus and a lack of creativity. You know, also, the proposed solution: focused daydreaming.

Right now we are living amidst the rise of AI, which is transforming the workplace. Despite AI's ostensible creative output, it lacks genuine discernment and consciousness – this is exactly what makes us humans (with our emotional, creative and critical intelligence) indispensable. It is also what will give us a key advantage in this new working world.

Making focused daydreaming a habit, rather than an afterthought or nice-to-have, is crucial for this exact reason. Implementing micro-habits, starting small with just a few minutes of focused daydreaming each day, facilitates gradual integration in your routine. Saying 'no' to non-essential tasks and setting communication boundaries are effective strategies to protect time for the real, meaningful work. Even in a resistant work environment, individuals can incorporate focused daydreaming through micro-breaks or by adopting the practice quietly.

A broader cultural shift towards focused daydreaming is the ideal goal here, fostering a workplace where creativity, accountability and improved mental wellbeing thrive. Embracing a positive mindset – backed by the scientific link between mind wandering and cognitive enhancement – solidifies focused daydreaming as a powerful tool for transforming work experiences and achieving success.

CHAPTER TEN

Fixing your focus at work

Focused daydreaming, in and of itself, is an invitation to direct your attention to your thinking. There are no hard and fast rules – your focus on thinking can be as tight or as loose as you want it to be. Though it's fair to say that when you're getting the most out of your thinking, you significantly increase your chances of finding focus, and ultimately implementing novel and creative ideas. To what degree is all up to you.

There are thousands of brilliant minds who are specialists in every possible area of neuroscience and applied psychology, and they're discovering more unique facts about our thinking hour by hour and day by day. At the most basic level, this book's aim has been to bring this knowledge to you in a way that's easy to understand and, most importantly, easy to act on.

You could say that my expertise is more hands-on and experiential, rather than scientific or academic. I've been very fortunate to have kept company with some exceptional people over the last 20 years. I've facilitated brainstorming sessions with Nobel Prize winners, incredible thinkers who have demonstrated the ability to apply creative thinking to change the world. I have worked with several royal families and governments and I've also had the opportunity to spend time with leading experts in science, business and humanitarian concerns.

Lately, I've learned that the majority of people are now ready for new ways of thinking and working that are based on sound and solid principles of how the brain works. They want tools that make sense and that are practical for increasing productivity both on a business and personal basis. Convincing them that focused daydreaming gives them the focus fix they need is now becoming possible. I hope this book has done the same for you so far.

Still, I do recognise that we must also be realistic. If you are a leader, a manager, or even the newest junior member of a company, there is a challenge behind bringing focused daydreaming into your team, without having to convince everyone of the science beforehand. Yes, you could provide each and every member of your team with a copy of this book, but as much as I would obviously champion this idea, there is another way.

What if you could get your colleagues to experience the benefits without even mentioning focused daydreaming! Here are a few techniques to get you started.

Overcoming failed brainstorming sessions

A question I am often asked when speaking with highly creative teams is: 'Why do our brainstorming sessions fail?' The answer is often very simple. They do not allow daydreaming to fit into the process. And yet to do so is both simple and natural. Just follow a process that empowers it. Here is a simple strategy…

Ask each person to prepare for a group session by brainstorming and working individually first. This is key. The idea is that all team members should clean out the corners of their mind to imagine as many potential solutions as they can before any group discussions actually take place.

If you wait until everyone is huddled together in a group to begin brainstorming, as is the norm, you'll find that the meeting becomes governed by group think (a state where harmony in the group is prized over debate surrounding the best ideas), potentially resulting in harmful evaluation apprehension (where people are afraid to share ideas for fear of looking stupid), social loafing (when individuals feel more comfortable contributing less because of the group setting) or production blocking (when a strong or dominant character blocks the ideas put forward by others).

Every individual has their own creative ideas, of course, but it often becomes all too easy in such an environment to be influenced by the thoughts of others. More forceful personalities can dominate the group when it comes to communicating their ideas, meaning that true brainstorming is inhibited and fewer innovative ideas are unleashed as a result. In contrast, when individuals work alone they aren't under any social pressures and are free to explore their thoughts (in other words, daydream) without any fear of criticism, and so even the quietest members of the group are able to contribute ideas when the time comes.

The next stage is to divide everyone into small groups in order to exchange ideas. What's the benefit of this? In a small group, people feel more able to speak up and contribute. It presents a safe space for them to share their thoughts as the dynamics are sheltered from an overwhelming environment where only the strongest communicator tends to dominate. Done this way, there is much greater objectivity and focus to the whole process and participants can work collectively to review their output, eliminate duplicates and select the ideas they want to take forward to the next stage. Ideally, you then allow a day or two for new ideas to incubate. Each member of the small group would have been exposed to new items of information during the group session. Thus they have more time and material to incubate, which will automatically give their minds time to create new connections.

The final stage is to draw everyone together for a large group meeting to discuss all the ideas generated and brought forward so far. Working collectively, the group should clarify, combine and refine ideas – as well as springboarding off existing ideas to create new ones!

If connections aren't clear between ideas, then the group should make some. The unique perspectives and associations of each individual and the time taken to incubate ideas contribute to the whole. As we've seen, conventional group brainstorming can be hugely detrimental to initial idea generation, mainly because conditions allow for the aforementioned undesirable psychological factors to proliferate.

This points us towards an important fact – you could have the best people and brainstorming techniques at your disposal, but if you haven't set up the environment and process correctly for proactive thinking, you're not going to get optimum results from your brainstorming sessions.

To do this, team members need to be given time to think, mull over and daydream – which, given some space, they will do naturally – without you even needing to mention focused daydreaming! This approach to brainstorming sessions combines the energy of everyone involved in a way that produces more profound insights, fresh perspectives and truly focused actions.

Reframe a challenge: say it differently – imagine it differently

Reframing is a transformative technique that stimulates our creative juices and drives us to deviate from our standard idea-generation patterns. Done correctly, the act of reframing key information or ideas can realign us with new, untapped starting points. Strikingly, even the act of rewording a problem statement can illuminate previously obscured solutions. This is truly a magic trick more of us could do with identifying and putting to use.

For maximum effectiveness, it's recommended to take an existing problem statement and, using a playful, open-minded approach, reframe it at least five times, switching verbs and nouns and studying it from all manner of angles.

This strategy pushes us towards the realms of focused daydreaming, encouraging us to let our minds meander into the unexplored territories we might not consider otherwise, fostering innovative thoughts and solutions as a result.

Posing new questions can be a valuable technique in this process. By morphing statements into enquiries, we inspire our minds to search for answers, a process that naturally leads us into the daydreaming state. For example, the statement 'our budget is limited' is static and uninspiring. In contrast, the question 'how might we expand our budget?' actively prompts us to creatively brainstorm potential new avenues to explore.

Furthermore, a precise refocusing technique involves alternating words and meanings within your current problem statement, triggering a cognitive shift. Changing 'increase sales' to 'develop sales' or 'give customers joy' subtly nudges your brain into different thinking pathways, fostering a richer daydreaming environment and fertile ground for your subconscious ideation.

The 'how-to' reframing approach is another great way to encourage focused daydreaming. Overwhelming problems can seem more manageable when phrased as possibilities – 'how to make staff happier' instead of 'staff morale is low'. From here, a brainstorming session can be entered into with an explorative mind, rather than a limited one.

It's believed that Henry Ford came up with the revolutionary assembly line by merely rephrasing a question from 'how do we bring the workers to the work?' to 'how do we bring the work to the workers?' – thus stumbling upon a workplace change which was essential to increased productivity (saving labour and increasing efficiency by allowing workers to put a piece of manufacturing together sequentially in one place).

Thus, it's clear to see that the tool of reframing doubles up as both a problem-solving and daydreaming aid. It takes a familiar problem and expresses it differently, forcing us to see it from a fresh perspective and so unveils richer possibilities in our focused daydreaming sessions.

Daydream to avoid assumptions

As we age, one of the reasons our creativity diminishes relates to our fixed beliefs and associated assumptions that then blind us from seeing the world objectively. Pablo Picasso, the Spanish artist, illustrated this point perfectly when he said, 'It took me four years to paint like Raphael but a lifetime to paint like a child.' Children can be free with their imagination as there aren't any assumptions holding them back. By eradicating our assumptions, we can rediscover this ability and experience the magic of creativity that we all knew as children. But how exactly do we begin to do that?

Innovative thinking often starts by questioning the status quo and other norms that have become accepted over time. These ingrained principles so often have come to dictate our actions and decisions, creating a buffer zone around our perspective and behaviour that reduces the potential to conceive creative and groundbreaking solutions. Yet it's crucially important to challenge our assumptions if we want to breed innovation.

Let's dive into this concept with an example. Imagine you're establishing a restaurant as a new business. The general assumptions you might consider would be that it needs to have a menu, food and staff. The power of focused daydreaming comes into play here as a way to challenge assumptions. Imagine yourself sitting in this hypothetical restaurant. Instead of a conventional restaurant setting, allow your mind to wander into unfamiliar territories. This is the crux of challenging the status quo – allowing your mind to reconceive a problem or challenge from a different perspective, and so produce new ideas as a result.

Daydreaming also allows your mind to take a break from reality and venture into a limitless landscape of possibilities. In this state, our mind does not feel the pressure to remain within the bounds of the 'normal' or 'accepted' ideas and thoughts. It's free to explore and create without constraints. It is the nature of mind wandering to produce a thinking experience that sits outside the 'box' of convention and assumption.

For instance, who said a restaurant must have a menu? In the daydream realm, customers could be bringing their own dish ideas for the chef to then execute. The staff, instead of waiting tables, could be actively interacting with customers, sharing today's special dishes verbally and having fruitful conversations as a result. Similarly, when we challenge the assumption that a restaurant has to offer food, our daydream mind could conjure up the concept of a 'bring-your-own-food' scenario. In this case, the business could be charging a venue fee. A situation where a restaurant runs without staff may seem preposterous, but in our daydream state, we could consider a self-service mode or vending machines that serve food or – in a utopian style – customers could serve each other.

We can expand the impact of daydreaming by reversing our assumptions – a potent way of fostering innovative ideas. For instance, restaurants are generally known to charge for the food they serve. What if, in your daydream state, you concoct a model where the food is free, but customers are charged for the time they spend in the restaurant? Challenging assumptions, coupled with focused daydreaming, can expose creative inputs and ideas that might seem unconventional but could end up disrupting an entire industry. That's not to say you need to follow each one to its end, but it's plain to see how this mode of thinking opens up a more original perspective.

To induce this daydreaming state in your team, you can make use of tools like guided imagery or storytelling to create a relaxed mental state. Create a scenario and allow yourself (and team members if in a group) to visualize and explore it in your minds. This exercises their creative freedoms and pushes them to challenge existing assumptions.

Doing this explicitly might call in a person's own self-monitor and restrict the creative vision that comes as a result... at least initially. Hence, it is important that these sessions focus on the storytelling aspect of the exercise rather than the potential outcomes of daydreaming as a creative tool. By consistently engaging in challenging assumptions and focused daydreaming, you are setting a stage for yourself and others to reach perceptual break-throughs, stretching creativity and allowing you to think without the box.

Shifting standpoints – focused daydreaming in play

Intentional daydreaming is incredibly powerful, but to make the most of it we must also think about the stance and mindset from which we begin to daydream. Our perspective – our personal point of reference – determines how we perceive problems and respond to challenges. Infused in every thought process we engage in, our viewpoint subtly influences the development and execution of our ideas.

Marcel Proust, the famed French novelist, once said: 'The real magic of discovery lies not in seeking new landscapes but in having new eyes.' And I must add, in seeing with new eyes, one invariably daydreams with a fresh outlook. When attempting to tackle a challenge, we generally default to our individual perspectives, taking into consideration our personal history, opinions and expertise. However, the simple act of shifting this perspective can result in an astonishing transformation in how creatively we approach issues. Shedding the weight of our own identity, we can suddenly experience fresh ideas, and so, novel solutions as well.

People with diverse backgrounds, experiences and professions see things in varied ways – an account manager sees a marketing problem differently than a customer service representative, and a finance person might bring an entirely fresh solution to a customer service issue. By adopting these alternative views, we not only broaden our understanding of the problem but also the possible solutions resulting from our focused daydreaming sessions.

Shifting perspective essentially engages the process of focused daydreaming from different standpoints. For instance, what would a politician do when facing the same predicament? How would a nurse tackle it? A child's approach? Or a bus driver's solution? Intellectually adopting these roles and their perspectives can guide your daydreaming to anchor yourself to less conventional insights, sparking unique, creative solutions to the problem – an approach that can be particularly effective once all familiar options have been exhausted and your thinking seems to be stuck in a rut.

Our perspectives are unique, defined by a vast array of factors from our upbringing, education, work experience to social conditions, personality, spiritual beliefs and much more. Each of these factors forms a lens through which we view the world. But the downside is that all of this is unalterably singular. Scoped within our experiences and knowledge, we encounter a bottleneck of creativity – predictable ideas and familiar solutions.

Thus, changing this standpoint becomes essential. Shifting our perspective during our daydreaming session can help us leap out of our narrow individual mindset, uncover unconventional solutions, escape from assumptions and force us to see our challenges from a fresh vantage point. From this angle, problems often take on entirely different forms, and the solutions appear more creative, and more fitting as well. This change of perspective, coupled with focused daydreaming, is key for creative problem solving.

What is important to remember is that at times we can be so attached to a situation that we see it only through our own lens. Conversely, shifting these lenses, changing our standpoint and engaging in focused daydreaming is where the magic truly happens. It provides us with a much-needed wider viewpoint – and a plethora of different perspectives – that ultimately fosters creativity and innovation.

Reversing the challenge – embracing the diametrical perspective

What do you think of when you think about the idea of 'reversing' something? You might associate it with words such as opposing, negating or cancelling. Maybe you even hear the beep, beep, beep of a car reversing backwards. From traffic jams to mathematics, this word is most commonly linked to the idea of a counter-effect, and may even broadly have negative connotations. Yet, when applied to critical and creative thinking, 'reversing' unfolds into a powerful, constructive tool to tilt, dissolve and re-establish the limited paradigms that hold us back in work and creative potential.

Imagine a situation where you are brainstorming ways to increase productivity within your team. A typical approach would naturally involve focusing on various strategies aimed at enhancing work performance. But what if we take a 'reverse' trajectory?

Ironically, by reframing the challenge to 'how to make the team less productive', we might tap into an entirely different thinking space. By focusing on ways to worsen the problem, we unconsciously craft a behavioural blueprint on actions and attitudes to avoid. Subsequently, reversing these actions sheds brighter light on novel, more effective solutions to the initial challenge. Suddenly, we're daydreaming in reverse, swinging between alternative realities but grounding ourselves deeper into the realms of practical wisdom. This technique is naturally reflective of focused daydreaming and the ways in which our subconscious can cook up ideas, even when – at the conscious level – it seems we are thinking about something else entirely.

The concept of shifting from 'what to do' to 'what not to do' can seem paradoxical, of course. However, identifying the aspects that can hinder your objective once again comes in the service of providing you with a broader perspective which yields real results. The shift involves stepping into the exact opposite direction, forcing you to view the challenge from a 180-degree angle that you can't reach when solely solution-focused.

Let's interpret 'reversing the challenge' in the context of a common business predicament: increasing customer acquisition. Rather than fixating on methods to 'gain' customers, consider the inverse: how to lose customers. Subsequently, evaluate the factors contributing to customer loss and invert them into strategies aimed at retaining and gaining customers.

Reverse brainstorming, by its nature, advocates for a philosophically contrapuntal thinking pattern. Instead of focusing energies on identifying solutions, it urges you to brainstorm ways to exacerbate the problem. This strategy, while initially jarring for some, spurs an oblique angle of creativity, awakening a surge of previously unconsidered ideas. Often it is actually easier to think of ways to make a problem worse rather than better – especially as such a goal releases the resistance and perfectionism that can sometimes be stifling to our thinking.

Let's follow these steps to perform a typical reverse brainstorming session:

1 Identifying the problem: take a close look at your issue. Using the previous example, we could consider the problem as: 'Increase customer acquisition'.

2 Reversing the problem: transform your challenge into its exact opposite. In this case, it would be: 'Lose more customers'.

3 Mapping the reverse problem: daydream and generate ideas and actions that could potentially lead to losing customers. This could include failing to establish brand trust, giving subpar customer service, or being outperformed by competitors.

4 Reversing the solutions: once you've identified diverse ways to lose customers (and essentially exacerbate your problem), you reverse these actions to create effective strategies. In this case, focusing on establishing brand trust, improving customer service and performing competitor analysis could lead you closer to your destination of increasing customer acquisition.

The transformative power of this technique lies in its efficacy to redefine perspective. It encourages a re-evaluation of existing problem-solving methods and offers access to unexplored dimensions of understanding. Furthermore, as focused daydreaming is a subconscious exercise, it impels individuals and teams to relax and envision the reversed scenario unconsciously. This process stirs the internal pot of creativity and brings them closer to cooking up really innovative outcomes.

Really, this is analogous to deconstructing a puzzle and then reassembling it – in the same way as this, reversing the challenge provides a unique panorama where anti-solutions evolve into concrete ideas for improvement. The essence of this technique lies in its simplicity and the improved view from an elevated perspective.

In conclusion, the process of reversing the challenge becomes a useful tool for enhancing the application of focused daydreaming. It allows the freedom to visualize, think and devise strategies from a unique standpoint. By stepping away from the norm and seeing problems from a flipped perspective, people can find unprecedented solutions.

In tandem, this alignment of contrastive thinking and focused daydreaming can generate a spectrum of creative ideas, ultimately contributing to the growth and success of any individual – or, indeed, any organization more broadly.

Finding focus and clarity through daydreaming

Focused daydreaming offers a unique space for employees to step away from the ceaseless flow of their daily tasks and gain perspective, clarity and ultimately find their focus.

As a tool, it provides an opportunity to untether minds from the constant pull of schedules, emails and assignments that are constantly fighting for our attention. In other words, this is a technique with the power to unshackle the mind – giving individuals the chance to explore what could be, rather than what just currently is.

This is why it's crucial we change the conversation around daydreaming at work. In a world driven by productivity and profits, daydreaming usually bears the brunt of being labelled as 'unproductive' or a 'waste of time'. But given the large amount of research that champions its benefits, it's high time to reframe daydreaming as an ally rather than an enemy. Remember, we are not promoting an infinite drift into oblivion but only a brief diversion, a short detour that re-energizes our minds for the onward journey.

One way to promote productive daydreaming within a team or to colleagues is to schedule regular 'daydreaming breaks'. You may prefer to call these 'thought experiments' if you feel that would be more palatable. The idea here is that during these periods of the day, your team drops their mundane duties and swims freely within the vast oceans of their minds. It's crucial to emphasize that these breaks aren't opportunities to wallow in non-work-related fantasies but rather to take a step back, re-evaluate and regroup.

A potential challenge here may be managing perceptions. No employee would want to be caught daydreaming by their superiors. Hence, it's crucial to foster an environment where daydreaming isn't seen as dereliction but as an encouraged activity. The key is to foster an open and accepting environment that endorses daydreaming.

Unveiling the benefits of focused daydreaming in a team setting could be approached strategically. One way to do this could be via 'daydreaming workshops'. These workshops would be dedicated sessions where employees can experience the advantages of focused daydreaming directly. As the leader, you can guide these sessions initially. Gradually, as everyone gets more comfortable, others can lead and share their journeys of daydreaming.

Let's remember, daydreaming is a personal journey. No one can dictate where a mind should wander, but what one can do is provide a jumping-off point and a springboard for that journey. One way to do it could be setting a theme for each session. For instance, 'What would our products look like in five years?' or 'What would we do if we knew we could not fail?' This focus will help channel the daydreams and shape them towards beneficial outcomes.

Fostering a storytelling culture is another powerful strategy that encourages daydreaming. Many times, imagining 'what could be' begins with hearing a scenario that doesn't exist yet. Your storytelling sessions could then evolve into collective group narrations where each member shares their thought processes and inferences.

Finally, let's not overlook the importance of cultivating a daydream-friendly environment. This environment could be both physical, like having quiet spaces for introspection, and psychological, fostering a culture that understands, respects and encourages the value of taking cognitive breaks for focused daydreaming.

The gentle drift towards focused daydreaming can sometimes be the only nudge teams need to break free of ingrained thinking and venture into the vast worlds of possibilities. So, let's find focus, clarity and ultimately success through daydreaming. You would be in good company...

Daydreaming is much more than idle fancy, and many successful business leaders have used it as a technique for problem solving, brainstorming and driving innovation. Here are some examples:

Warren Buffett: Known for his sage wisdom in business and investment, Buffet reportedly spends 80 per cent of his day reading and thinking. He has been quoted as saying, 'I insist on a lot of time being spent, almost every day, to just sit and think. I do it because I like this kind of life.' Clearly, part of Buffett's success can be attributed to the amount of focused daydreaming he does daily.

Bill Gates: The co-founder of Microsoft reportedly takes a week off twice a year just for reflection and reading. Referred to as 'Think Weeks', these practices emphasize the value of abandoning daily routines to encourage free thought and creativity, essentially promoting focused daydreaming.

Sir Richard Branson: The adventurous entrepreneur has often spoken about the importance of switching off and daydreaming to fuel creativity. 'I always keep a notebook in my pocket,' shared Branson, implying that his daydreaming often leads to ideas worth jotting down. He also states that you should, 'open your calendar and schedule time just to dream.'

Sara Blakely: Billionaire and founder of shapewear empire SPANX® credits her visualization practice as the top factor in SPANX's success. Blakely states that the key to successful visualization is specificity. Visualization is a form of daydreaming, with the specificity being the intentional direction.

Elon Musk: Musk, the forward-thinking entrepreneur behind SpaceX and Tesla, is famous for his futuristic daydreams. His mother Maye Musk stated, 'He goes into his brain and then you just see he is in another world. He still does that. Now I just leave him be because I know he is designing a new rocket or something.'

These are only a few examples, but it's incredibly clear that focused daydreaming isn't idle time. Instead, it's an opportunity for innovative ideas to surface, for the brain to rearrange information, and for leaders to channel their powers of strong critical and creative thinking.

Summary: perspective reimagined

In today's feverish business climate, where the emphasis is often on speed and efficiency, the concept of focused daydreaming may seem counterintuitive. Popular perception typically deems daydreaming as a lapse in productivity, but through reframing and a closer examination, we can recognize its potential for fostering innovation and creativity.

Organizational leaders across various hierarchy levels can harness this potential and encourage a culture of daydreaming within their teams. Still, they may face a critical challenge – how to introduce the notion of focused daydreaming without the need to thoroughly elaborate on the science behind it. To circumvent this challenge, reframing such exercises as visualization or thought experiments can facilitate acceptance among colleagues.

Furthermore, restructuring traditional brainstorming sessions to accommodate daydreaming, employing techniques such as preparing in isolation, small group exchanges and incubation periods followed by large group discussions can be instrumental. This method can encourage individual creativity and promote focused strategies while subtly incorporating daydreaming in the process.

While all these daydreaming practices can offer immense value, it is essential to create an enabling environment within organizations. This environment could encourage 'daydreaming breaks', foster an open and accepting culture and endorse 'focused daydreaming workshops'. Also, promoting storytelling culture and creating daydream-friendly spaces can further enhance outcomes.

In conclusion, focused daydreaming is an under-utilized yet incredibly powerful tool within the business setting, especially in an era filled with AI and automation. If cultivated and fostered correctly, it can be a radical avenue for individual and organizational creativity, innovation and focused strategic direction.

CHAPTER ELEVEN

Soaring swans

How did we get here?

Well, we're nearly at the end of our journey to fix our focus. As simple as that mission might seem on the surface, the challenge it poses for so many of us is very real and – more often than not – confounding. If this book has served one purpose, I hope it's been to show you the many angles and perspectives from which focus itself can be viewed. While we often think of focus as little more than a form of concentration, the truth is much more nuanced. No wonder, then, that the solution seems a little unconventional as well.

Still, let's take some time to think more deeply for a minute. What do we really mean when we talk about focus? I don't just mean in terms of its literal definition, but in the actual manifestation of it in our own lives. Sure, we can all agree that focus is something we could use more of. But when we say we want to 'fix our focus', what we're really saying is that we want to feel more connected and successful at work. Obviously, feeling distractible and mentally exhausted does not produce that sense of connection.

I would argue that we ultimately associate focus with that sensation of enjoying our work. We're rarely more focused than when we're immersed in a task we truly enjoy and feel motivated to complete. As we've touched on already, creativity is so often the energy that makes such a state possible. Even those who do not view themselves as 'creative' are most often dealing with some form of innovative or idea-centric work when truly in the flow of a task or project – regardless of whether they'd characterize it that way themselves.

The metacognitive necessity

It might still seem paradoxical: how can a process traditionally tied to inattention and distraction be considered conducive to focus? In this context, the answer is deep-seated in an evolved understanding of what focus means.

Typically, we frame focus as a form of exclusive attention centred on a single task or subject. However, this is a rather limited perspective; a product of industrial-age thinking, where focus was more about repetitiveness and less about awareness. Today, in the age of AI and automation, focus needs to be seen in the context of meta-cognition, or the ability to think about our thinking.

In this new perspective of focus pertaining to the sphere of work, education and learning, it is no longer restricted to 'concentrating on a linear task'. Focus evolves to a broadened understanding of 'the capacity to perceive the bigger picture, to estimate the interplay of ideas, facts and emotions, to approach problem solving from multiple angles, and to master resilience and emotional intelligence. Embracing this perspective of focus cultivates the necessary skills needed in the current and future workforces: creativity, critical thinking, resilience and character development.

As such, the act of focused daydreaming is the core of the new cognitive revolution, as it provides the cerebral grounds to cultivate this evolved form of focus. When allowed to wander in the valleys of our thoughts in a structured manner, our minds generate fresh connections, unexpected insights and innovative solutions.

As we have learnt, daydreaming is not the antagonist of focus; it is, in fact, the enabler. When strategically cultivated, focused daydreaming can function as a honing mechanism. By unlocking the mind's potential to rearrange and reimagine ideas, it trains us to expand our creative cognitive capacities and problem-solving skills.

More importantly, it brings an element of curiosity, openness and resilience to your mental state, all of which are cornerstones of this new perspective on focus. It cultivates the ability to find stability amidst disturbance, originality amidst conformity, and focus amidst diversity. It paves the way for introspection, self-awareness and empathy.

Contrary to the belief that daydreaming detracts from action-oriented work, in a redefined cognitive landscape, it is a tool for richer, deeper and more embodied work outcomes. It motivates individuals to question, comprehend and explore information rather than merely memorizing or duplicating it. In this sense, it is not just about teaching people to be diligent workers, but also cultivating them as creative thinkers, innovators and empathetic leaders.

'The Focus Fix' is the shift from an industrial-age focus of singularity and repetition to a neurocognitive focus of diversity, creativity and emotional maturity. Focused daydreaming serves as the key to unlocking and making the most out of this shift.

Doing less, succeeding more

Really, this has been the key premise of the whole book. The idea that when we give ourselves more time to be unfocused, and do so in a strategic way, we actually improve our ability to prioritize and focus during the times we are working – while also actually bringing more clarity and precision to our overall neurological functioning.

Needless to say, this is a paradigm shift for most of us. It challenges the mindset that we can only achieve good work through constant, strenuous effort. Indeed, this fallacy is exactly what has cultivated many toxic working cultures in which presence at work is assumed to equal productivity.

A wealth of scientific research shows that – far from enabling good work – continuous focus without respite actually has adverse effects on our prefrontal cortex (the brain's executive hub). It is this pressure which, over time, leads to burnout and other mental health challenges.

This is why focused daydreaming is such an effective strategy for genuinely achieving more without needing to spend more time working. The benefits of regular breaks as a pre-emptive measure against burnout are substantiated by research; with the addition of focused daydreaming, time away from work becomes even more effective, boosting the cognitive effects of this time away and allowing your subconscious to incubate new ideas.

As a mental state, creativity comes naturally paired with dynamism and energy. When we leave our minds free to wander, we give our subconscious mind time to play and gain momentum, which can then be translated into fresh ideas and perspectives.

Education and the metacognitive revolution

We've already touched somewhat on how the workplace of the future might shift and change – something also worth mentioning is the educational landscape. There is broad consensus across the educational field that metacognitive skills – particularly creativity, critical thinking, problem solving, and resilience – will be of utmost importance for the classrooms of the future.

The higher demand for these skills is the direct result of the exponential technological advancements led primarily by Artificial Intelligence (AI). These developments are set to invariably change our notion of traditional work, moving us away from the Industrial Age processes to a cognitive-based structure. In this scenario, daydreaming, which is often frowned upon in the schooling system, could provide the missing link that allows us to harness our true potential in the AI-dominated future.

Traditionally, daydreaming has been pushed into the corners of impracticality. Considered an undesirable behaviour in schools, it is usually associated with a lack of focus, inattentiveness, and thus as a waste of productive energy that could be harnessed in a more structured manner.

However, this conventional belief is an antiquated echo of Industrial Age thinking where standardization and replication were the nodes of progress. A McKinsey report, Building Workforce Skills at Scale (2021), constructs a similar sentiment. Their research highlights that as AI automates routine tasks, it will create an emphatic shift in the analytical dominion of human cognition to skills that machines can't replicate or replace: creativity, empathy, emotional intelligence, critical thinking and complex problem solving.

The Organization for Economic Co-operation and Development (OECD) is an intergovernmental organization with 38 member countries, founded in 1961 to stimulate economic progress and world trade. The OECD report 'Skills for 2030' argues that while AI is fast replacing many routine jobs, it struggles with positions requiring creativity, innovative approaches and original ideas (OECD, nd). This report brings the relevance of metacognitive skills for the future workforce into sharp focus. However, it also points out a glaring challenge: our education system is not sufficiently equipped to create these nurtured minds of the future.

So, where does focused daydreaming factor into all of this? Part of the answer lies in the National Foundation for Educational Research (NFER) report 'The Skills Imperative', which asserts that creativity, critical thinking, teamwork, problem solving and resilience will be critical for future jobs (NFER, nd). These are precisely the skills one can cultivate and polish during the process of structured daydreaming. By making room for the mind to wander, to connect and reconnect disparate information, to imagine and to create, we can offer learners an internal playground to nurture these skills.

Strategically, focused daydreaming provides a wholesome neural diet of exploration, freedom and creativity. It allows the brain to venture into unexplored terrains of possibilities, encouraging connections between certain pathways that may not be instantly obvious. This, in turn, cultivates resilience, a metacognitive skill that is critical in a future dominated by unforeseen changes and challenges.

Mastering the art of focused daydreaming requires deliberate efforts and a shift in mindset. Schools and institutions will need to wean away from the outdated paradigm that sees daydreaming simply as a distraction. It's time to wake up to the potential of daydreaming. By weaving it into our educational and professional environments, we can foster a generation of creative thinkers and problem solvers capable of not just surviving, but truly thriving in the new world order. In an age where machines are set to rule the roost, an old, clichéd, much-maligned practice known as daydreaming may well be the secret weapon that keeps humans in the driving seat. And just like that, AI and daydreaming, two polarities of the cognitive spectrum, could become the most unlikely allies in a brave new world of work.

Expanding the scope of learning

The nature of learning and acquiring skills has to adapt not only to the technological developments but also to this shift in perception towards daydreaming. Encouraging daydreaming doesn't involve an erasure of existing structures of education, but rather augmenting them in alignment with this more expansive view of cognition.

Interestingly, a large part of this learning involves giving space and time for focused daydreaming. With a conscious and calculated approach to daydreaming, students are encouraged to let their minds wander, to let thoughts flow freely and to question the why, the how and the what-if of their learning. This seemingly unstructured activity trains the brain in problem solving, decision making, and critical thinking – all instrumental skills in the confluence of idea generation, creativity and innovation.

As we move into a future where AI could be responsible for many of our existing job roles, the ability to think divergently and creatively will set humans apart. At the same time, AI can be instrumental in building an environment that supports these cognitive skills. In this landscape,

AI and automations are not the adversaries of human cognition, but rather powerful allies that can help us to both harness and focus our creative abilities.

In essence, the key to preparing all of us for the future lies not in rivalling AI on tasks it can do more accurately and efficiently, but in nurturing the elements of cognition that are uniquely human: the ability to brainstorm unique ideas, experience emotions, engage in critical introspection and apply knowledge creatively. It is not a competition; it is a co-production, where AI and human cognition can fuel each other, nurturing an ecosystem of productiveness and creativity.

The sooner we accept and adapt to this new normal where higher cognitive skills become not an advantageous extra but a necessary requisite, the better positioned we will be. Moreover, to squander the possibility of fulfilling the tremendous cognitive capacity that daydreaming holds would be to neglect the full potential we have by nature. From fostering resilience and resourcefulness to sharpening our problem-solving skills and widening our creative horizon, focused daydreaming could be the missing piece of the puzzle in an AI-dominated society.

In the grand scheme of things, focused daydreaming is an unexplored conduit of human potential and the key to unlocking the metacognitive revolution. As we head into a future shadowed by AI, where the onus of a monotony of tasks is shifted away from humans, focused daydreaming may well be our path to standing our cognitive ground, to reimagining education and, indeed, to rethinking the very purpose of human cognition.

From boiling frog to soaring swan

Returning to our frog metaphor from the opening of this book, it's clear our work culture has been steadily heated like the proverbial pot of boiling water. Similarly, the dominance of digital technology in both our professional and personal lives has become so prevalent that we've barely noticed the escalation. The narrative of the boiling frog is a stark reminder of how we have, like the frog, failed to react to these gradual but serious changes.

These are not merely fluctuations of focus in a workday, but an extensive shift, a collective slowing down of mental sharpness due to relentless digital distractions and an unhealthy novelty-seeking behaviour induced by constant online stimulation. We've adapted so instinctively to this chaotic digital noise that our minds, much like the boiling frog, are in peril of becoming too accustomed, too oblivious, losing our natural threat detectors amidst incessant technological intrusion.

To lift ourselves out of this metaphorical pot, and to regain the mental clarity and focus that is only ours to reclaim, it is time to consciously acknowledge the escalating changes, the constant rise in digital distractions, and the relentless need for connectivity. It is time to step off the relentless conveyor belt of unending emails, video calls and social media notifications. It is time to lower the flame, reduce the noise and rediscover focus amidst the technological flurry. It is time to move away from being the slowly boiled frog and instead to be like the swan, soaring above to see the bigger picture where we can then navigate towards a better future.

A final word

We all want to be more successful. Yet, in the thick of the chaos of the modern day, more often than not we'd settle simply for feeling more focused. If this book has shown you anything, I hope it's that – with commitment to this technique – you can have both.

Focused daydreaming is not a quick fix. Implementing daydream breaks here and there won't immediately transform your life. But, if you're serious about committing to this new way of working – and ditching Busy Fool Syndrome for good – it really does have the power to help you reconnect with the focus that has been stolen and divided by our demanding working culture.

What's more, finding clarity in the chaos is not only helpful, it's liberating! While so many people are burning out and giving up, focused daydreaming has the power to help you rediscover the joy of the everyday. We can no longer afford to ignore this invaluable tool by repressing a cognitive function that is actually integral to our ability to think clearly and well.

Amidst the clamour for productivity hacks and elevated efficiency, focused daydreaming stands out as something accessible and genuine. It's not just about getting more done; it's about doing the right things with a heightened sense of purpose and creative flair. By embracing focused daydreaming, we can carve out moments of respite in our hectic lives, allowing our minds to recharge and rejuvenate, and at the same time reap the benefits of our brain at its best. So, what are you waiting for? It looks like the perfect day for a daydream.

Where to go next

To help you get started on your journey, visit ChrisGriffiths. com for additional resources, templates, articles and downloads.

REFERENCES

Introduction

Cambridge Dictionary (2019) MINDSET: meaning in the Cambridge English Dictionary, Cambridge.org, https://dictionary.cambridge.org/dictionary/english/mindset (archived at https://perma.cc/3ZAT-4TEQ)

CEBR (2023) Leading economic forecasts and analysis | CEBR. (2023) The Independent – Work-related stress and burnout costing UK economy £28bn per year, research shows, CEBR, https://cebr.com/reports/the-independent-work-related-stress-and-burnout-costing-uk-economy-28bn-per-year-research-shows/ (archived at https://perma.cc/3NLW-WUHN)

Fallows, J (2009) Guest-post wisdom on frogs, *The Atlantic*, www.theatlantic.com/technology/archive/2009/07/guest-post-wisdom-on-frogs/21789/ (archived at https://perma.cc/SM7K-MBEW)

Gallup (2022) State of the Global Workplace Report, www.gallup.com/workplace/349484/state-of-the-global-workplace-2022-report.aspx (archived at https://perma.cc/WQ7R-7L59)

Mayfield, M, Mayfield, J and Ma, K Q (2020) Innovation matters: creative environment, absenteeism, and job satisfaction, *Journal of Organizational Change Management*, ahead-of-print(ahead-of-print) https://doi.org/10.1108/jocm-09-2019-0285 (archived at https://perma.cc/P292-TN8R)

Microsoft (2021) Research proves your brain needs breaks, www.microsoft.com/en-us/worklab/work-trend-index/brain-research (archived at https://perma.cc/ALB8-ACMT)

Office for National Statistics (nd) UK Whole Economy: Output per hour worked % change per annum SA, www.ons.gov.uk/employmentandlabourmarket/peopleinwork/labourproductivity/timeseries/lzvd/prdy (archived at https://perma.cc/BA85-KMRP)

Puiu, T (2015) Your smartphone is millions of times more powerful that all of NASA's combined computing in 1969, ZME Science, www.zmescience.com/feature-post/technology-articles/computer-science/smartphone-power-compared-to-apollo-432/ (archived at https://perma.cc/YT8D-UALG)

Ricoh Europe (2022) Employers face 'creativity' challenge, not worker apathy, www.ricoh-europe.com/news-events/news/employers-face-creativity-challenge-not-worker-apathy/ (archived at https://perma.cc/MK29-DVEN)

Chapter 1: A surprising way to find focus

Andrews, S, Ellis, D A, Shaw, H and Piwek, L (2015) Beyond Self-Report: Tools to Compare Estimated and Real-World Smartphone Use, PLOS ONE, **10** (10), p.e0139004, https://doi.org/10.1371/journal.pone.0139004 (archived at https://perma.cc/8W9Y-ACKB)

Bench, S and Lench, H (2013) On the Function of Boredom, *Behavioral Sciences*, **3** (3), pp. 459–72, https://doi.org/10.3390/bs3030459 (archived at https://perma.cc/JSP9-E2FD)

Christoff, K, Gordon, A M, Smallwood, J, Smith, R and Schooler, J W (2009) Experience sampling during fMRI reveals default network and executive system contributions to mind wandering, *Proceedings of the National Academy of Sciences*, **106** (21) www.sciencedaily.com/releases/2009/05/090511180702.htm (archived at https://perma.cc/BTA5-ER49)

Duke, É and Montag, C (2017) Smartphone addiction and beyond: initial insights on an emerging research topic and its relationship to internet addiction, *Internet Addiction*, pp. 359–72, https://doi.org/10.1007/978-3-319-46276-9_21 (archived at https://perma.cc/5D97-3WNB)

Duke, K, Ward, A, Gneezy, A and Bos, M (2018) Having your smartphone nearby takes a toll on your thinking (even when it's silent and facedown) *Harvard Business Review*, https://hbr.org/2018/03/having-your-smartphone-nearby-takes-a-toll-on-your-thinking (archived at https://perma.cc/6BTY-22BP)

Gregory, E (2022) What does it mean to be neurodivergent? *Forbes Health*, http://www.forbes.com/health/mind/what-is-neurodivergent/ (archived at https://perma.cc/L76C-CGE9)

Hyland, K (2023) Academic publishing and the attention economy, *Journal of English for Academic Purposes*, **64**, pp. 101253–101253, https://doi.org/10.1016/j.jeap.2023.101253 (archived at https://perma.cc/CV3T-FBAC)

Kraus, C, Ganger, S, Losak, J, Hahn, A, Savli, M, Kranz, GS, Baldinger, P, Windischberger, C, Kasper, S and Lanzenberger, R (2014) Gray matter and intrinsic network changes in the posterior cingulate cortex after selective serotonin reuptake inhibitor intake, *NeuroImage*, **84**, pp. 236–244, https://doi.org/10.1016/j.neuroimage.2013.08.036 (archived at https://perma.cc/Y4K2-X8BF)

Mark, G, Gudith, D and Klocke, U (2008) The cost of interrupted work, *Proceeding of the twenty-sixth annual CHI conference on Human factors in computing systems – CHI '08*, https://doi.org/10.1145/1357054.1357072 (archived at https://perma.cc/C58Z-PDZU)

Medlicott, C (2022) Techniques which talk to neurodivergent brains, *Ayoa*, http://www.ayoa.com (archived at https://perma.cc/7ZQM-PP2L). http://www.ayoa.com/ourblog/techniques-which-talk-to-neurodivergent-brains/ (archived at https://perma.cc/HE85-8FPU)

Mooneyham, B W and Schooler, J W (2013) The costs and benefits of mind-wandering: A review, *Canadian Journal of Experimental*

Psychology / Revue canadienne de psychologie expérimentale,
67 (1), pp. 11–18, https://doi.org/10.1037/a0031569 (archived
at https://perma.cc/S58X-UDWY)

Petrone, P (2018) The skills companies need most in 2019 – and
how to learn them, LinkedIn, www.linkedin.com/business/
learning/blog/top-skills-and-courses/the-skills-companies-
need-most-in-2019-and-how-to-learn-them (archived at
https://perma.cc/2GUX-CAQZ)

Ukkola-Vuoti, L et al (2013) Genome-wide copy number variation
analysis in extended families and unrelated individuals
characterized for musical aptitude and creativity in music, *PLoS
ONE*, 8 (2), p. e56356, https://doi.org/10.1371/journal.
pone.0056356 (archived at https://perma.cc/P7HW-VSXA)

Weir, K (2022) The science behind creativity, *American
Psychological Association*, http://www.apa.org/
monitor/2022/04/cover-science-creativity (archived at https://
perma.cc/ES3T-SFSC)

West, M J, Somer, E and Eigsti, I-M (2022) Immersive and
maladaptive daydreaming and divergent thinking in autism
spectrum disorders, *Imagination, Cognition and Personality*,
42 (4), p. 027623662211298, https://doi.org/10.1177/
02762366221129819 (archived at https://perma.cc/BSZ5-RRS2)

Wheelwright, T (2022) Cell phone behavior survey: are people
addicted to their phones? *reviews.org*, www.reviews.org/mobile/
cell-phone-addiction/ (archived at https://perma.cc/2QCQ-
N4CA)

Wigmore, I (nd) Attention economy, www.techtarget.com/
whatis/definition/attention-economy (archived at
https://perma.cc/T7ZW-BUBE)

World Economic Forum (2023) The Future of Jobs Report 2023,
World Economic Forum. www.weforum.org/reports/the-future-
of-jobs-report-2023/digest (archived at https://perma.cc/8KEN-
WB3Z)

Chapter 2: Battling burnout in a connected world

Brod, C (1984) *Technostress: The human cost of the computer revolution*, Addison-Wesley Reading, Mass

Davis, P (2019) Is burnout real? The answer is yes, *Forbes*, http://www.forbes.com/sites/pauladavislaack/2019/06/06/is-burnout-real-the-answer-is-yes/ (archived at https://perma.cc/TC5X-3ZQB)

Gallup (2023) State of the Global Workplace Report, Gallup.com, www.gallup.com/workplace/349484/state-of-the-global-workplace.aspx (archived at https://perma.cc/8Z26-F4DB)

Kahneman, D (2011) *Thinking, Fast and Slow*, Allen Lane, London

Microsoft (2023) Work Trend Index | Will AI Fix Work? www.microsoft.com (archived at https://perma.cc/CGN7-RLRJ). www.microsoft.com/en-us/worklab/work-trend-index/will-ai-fix-work (archived at https://perma.cc/3GHK-PKV6)

Newport, C (2022) It's time to embrace slow productivity, *The New Yorker*, www.newyorker.com/culture/office-space/its-time-to-embrace-slow-productivity (archived at https://perma.cc/XM9L-4YZT)

Noy, S et al (2023) Experimental evidence on the productivity effects of generative artificial intelligence, https://economics.mit.edu/sites/default/files/inline-files/Noy_Zhang_1.pdf (archived at https://perma.cc/76PC-TPBL)

Prane (2023) 'Gruelling' work intensity a growing problem in 'burnt out Britain', new TUC report shows, TUC, www.tuc.org.uk (archived at https://perma.cc/79P2-88HJ). www.tuc.org.uk/news/gruelling-work-intensity-growing-problem-burnt-out-britain-new-tuc-report-shows (archived at https://perma.cc/N7NY-J8PP)

Sharma, K (2023) What is Technostress? (+how to deal with it), Whatfix, https://whatfix.com/blog/beat-workplace-technostress/ (archived at https://perma.cc/F8SU-3LL5)

UiPath Investor Relations. (2023) New global survey reveals nearly 60% of workers believe ai-powered automation improves job fulfillment, https://ir.uipath.com/news/detail/289/new-global-survey-reveals-nearly-60-of-workers-believe (archived at https://perma.cc/7P89-H8Y8)

Vallance, C (2023) AI could replace equivalent of 300 million jobs – report, BBC News, http://www.bbc.co.uk/news/technology-65102150 (archived at https://perma.cc/U4QG-A5YU)

World Health Organization (2019) Burn-out an 'occupational phenomenon': International classification of diseases, World Health Organization, www.who.int/news/item/28-05-2019-burn-out-an-occupational-phenomenon-international-classification-of-diseases (archived at https://perma.cc/6RXS-4E9A)

Chapter 3: Unlock your untapped creative potential

Brandes, L (2020) Henri Matisse – the Art of Daydream, *L'officiel*, www.lofficiel.at/en/art-and-culture/henri-matisse-the-art-of-daydream

Fries, A R (2009) *Daydreams at Work: Wake up your creative powers*, Capital Books, Sterling, VA

History Extra (2020) The Brontës: the unfortunate and unlikely tale of the world's 'greatest literary sisters', www.historyextra.com/period/victorian/bronte-sisters-anne-charlotte-emily-who-were-they-house-famous-write-books

Hossenfelder, S (2015) Head Trip, *Scientific American*, **313** (3), pp. 46–49, https://doi.org/10.1038/scientificamerican0915-46 (archived at https://perma.cc/WC64-BUED)

Kernan, M (1982) The man who launched the space age, *Washington Post*, 19 Sep, www.washingtonpost.com/archive/lifestyle/1982/09/19/the-man-who-launched-the-space-age/ (archived at https://perma.cc/B2GS-M8SN)

Nix, E (2018) Did an apple really fall on Isaac Newton's head? *HISTORY*, www.history.com/news/did-an-apple-really-fall-on-isaac-newtons-head (archived at https://perma.cc/K5WV-TUUS)

Ross, R (2017) Eureka! The Archimedes Principle, *Live Science*, www.livescience.com/58839-archimedes-principle.html (archived at https://perma.cc/7NEG-QG8S)

Stern, D P (2016) Robert Goddard and his rockets, pwg.gsfc.nasa.gov, https://pwg.gsfc.nasa.gov/stargaze/Sgoddard.htm (archived at https://perma.cc/ZSJ4-YWMD)

Stetka, B (2021) Spark creativity with Thomas Edison's napping technique, *Scientific American*, www.scientificamerican.com/article/thomas-edisons-naps-inspire-a-way-to-spark-your-own-creativity (archived at https://perma.cc/32VV-UJ53)

Thea (2018) Is daydreaming good for creativity? Hopper and Matisse have the answer, *The Charmed Studio Blog*, https://thecharmedstudio.com/matisse-windows-daydreaming (archived at https://perma.cc/4NVS-HQFF)

Thompson, H (1966) Quiet murders suit Miss Christie; Visiting writer still prefers to keep crime in family, *The New York Times*, 27 Oct, www.nytimes.com/1966/10/27/archives/quiet-murders-suit-miss-christie-visiting-writer-still-prefers-to.html (archived at https://perma.cc/P2WX-F78V)

Wickelgren, I (2011) Delivered in a daydream: 7 great achievements that arose from a wandering mind, *Scientific American*, www.scientificamerican.com/article/achievements-of-wandering-minds/ (archived at https://perma.cc/2E5M-8NMT)

Zedelius, C M, Protzko, J, Broadway, J M and Schooler, J W (2020) What types of daydreaming predict creativity? Laboratory and experience sampling evidence, *Psychology of Aesthetics, Creativity, and the Arts*, https://doi.org/10.1037/aca0000342 (archived at https://perma.cc/W7SJ-EXND)

Chapter 4: The misinterpreted mental voyage

Baird, B et al (2012) Inspired by distraction: Mind wandering facilitates creative incubation, *Psychological Science*, **23** (10), pp. 1117–22 https://doi.org/10.1177/0956797612446024 (archived at https://perma.cc/9Y89-VHL9)

Fox, D (2008) The secret life of the brain, *New Scientist*, www.newscientist.com/article/mg20026811-500-the-secret-life-of-the-brain/ (archived at https://perma.cc/7UM8-NNVV)

Hatano, A, Ogulmus, C, Shigemasu, H and Murayama, K (2022) Thinking about thinking: People underestimate how enjoyable and engaging just waiting is, *Journal of Experimental Psychology: General*, https://doi.org/10.1037/xge0001255 (archived at https://perma.cc/HX6V-9MKX)

Johnston, M V et al (2009) Plasticity and injury in the developing brain, *Brain and Development*, **31** (1), pp. 1–10, https://doi.org/10.1016/j.braindev.2008.03.014 (archived at https://perma.cc/T4BU-SQVT)

Killingsworth, M A and Gilbert, D T (2010) A wandering mind is an unhappy mind, *Science*, **330** (6006), p. 932, https://doi.org/10.1126/science.1192439 (archived at https://perma.cc/4NNV-9P6K)

Land, G and Jarman B (1992) *Breakpoint and Beyond: Mastering the future today*, Harpercollins Publishers

Nastasi, J, Tassistro, I B and Gravina, N (2023) Breaks and productivity: An exploratory analysis, *Journal of Applied Behavior Analysis*, https://doi.org/10.1002/jaba.995 (archived at https://perma.cc/38KZ-D8NQ)

Nguyen, N D et al (2024) Cortical reactivations predict future sensory responses, *Nature*, **625** (7993), pp. 110–18, https://doi.org/10.1038/s41586-023-06810-1 (archived at https://perma.cc/VA6T-MGCJ)

Science Daily (2009) Brain's problem-solving function at work when we daydream, www.sciencedaily.com/releases/2009/05/090511180702.htm (archived at https://perma.cc/BTA5-ER49)

Sleep Foundation (2021) Maladaptive daydreaming: symptoms, diagnosis, and tips, www.sleepfoundation.org/mental-health/maladaptive-daydreaming (archived at https://perma.cc/EKL8-YFPT)

Suttie, J (2021) What daydreaming does to your mind, *Greater Good Magazine*, https://greatergood.berkeley.edu/article/item/what_daydreaming_does_to_your_mind (archived at https://perma.cc/R3FQ-KG8T)

Westgate, E C and Wilson, T D (2016) With a little help for our thoughts: Making it easier to think for pleasure, *APA PsycNet*, http://www.erinwestgate.com/uploads/7/6/4/1/7641726/westgatewilsongilbert.emotion.pdf (archived at https://perma.cc/6WGG-NF27)

Wilson, T D et al (2014) Just think: The challenges of the disengaged mind, *Science*, **345** (6192), pp. 75–77, https://doi.org/10.1126/science.1250830 (archived at https://perma.cc/K8W2-98RX)

Zedelius, C M, Protzko, J, Broadway, J M and Schooler, J W (2020) What types of daydreaming predict creativity? Laboratory and experience sampling evidence, *Psychology of Aesthetics, Creativity, and the Arts*, https://doi.org/10.1037/aca0000342 (archived at https://perma.cc/W7SJ-EXND)

Chapter 5: Doing less to achieve more

Baird, B et al (2012) Inspired by distraction: Mind wandering facilitates creative incubation, *Psychological Science*, **23** (10), pp. 1117–22, https://doi.org/10.1177/0956797612446024 (archived at https://perma.cc/9Y89-VHL9)

Cleveland Clinic (2023) The amygdala: A small part of your brain's biggest abilities, https://my.clevelandclinic.org/health/body/24894-amygdala (archived at https://perma.cc/HY9B-CYUQ)

Davis, J (2015) Zoning out can make you more productive, *Harvard Business Review*, https://hbr.org/2015/06/zoning-out-can-make-you-more-productive (archived at https://perma.cc/V5UX-YDAD)

Demsky, C A, Fritz, C, Hammer, L B and Black, A E (2019) Workplace incivility and employee sleep: The role of rumination and recovery experiences, *Journal of Occupational Health Psychology*, **24** (2), pp. 228–40, https://doi.org/10.1037/ocp0000116 (archived at https://perma.cc/9NNW-Q77W)

Farnsworth, B (2020) A beginner's guide to neuroscience, iMotions, https://imotions.com/blog/learning/research-fundamentals/beginners-guide-neuroscience/ (archived at https://perma.cc/L8PC-EEW2)

Golkar, A, Johansson, E, Kasahara, M, Osika, W, Perski, A and Savic, I (2014) The influence of work-related chronic stress on the regulation of emotion and on functional connectivity in the brain, PLOS ONE, https://journals.plos.org/plosone/article?id=10.1371/journal.pone.0104550 (archived at https://perma.cc/P3RC-X3YP)

Heinemann, L V and Heinemann, T (2017) Burnout Research: Emergence and scientific investigation of a contested diagnosis, *SAGE Open*, **7** (1), p. 215824401769715, https://doi.org/10.1177/2158244017697154 (archived at https://perma.cc/6RGB-3NHG)

Kühnel, J and Sonnentag, S (2010) How long do you benefit from vacation? A closer look at the fade-out of vacation effects, *Journal of Organizational Behavior*, **32** (1), pp. 125–43, https://doi.org/10.1002/job.699 (archived at https://perma.cc/WB2Y-7JCP)

Liston, C, McEwen, B S and Casey, B J (2009) Psychosocial stress reversibly disrupts prefrontal processing and attentional control, *Proceedings of the National Academy of Sciences*, **106** (3), pp. 912–17, https://doi.org/10.1073/pnas.0807041106 (archived at https://perma.cc/3DKY-BKEH)

Michel, A (2016) Burnout and the brain, *APS Observer*, **29** (2), www.psychologicalscience.org/observer/burnout-and-the-brain (archived at https://perma.cc/M8HA-FMGW)

News Medical (2021) Visual imagination motivates people to engage in pleasurable and achievement-oriented activities, www.news-medical.net/news/20210823/Visual-imagination-motivates-people-to-engage-in-pleasurable-and-achievement-oriented-activities.aspx (archived at https://perma.cc/UF2K-BKXJ)

Puente-Díaz, R and Cavazos-Arroyo, J (2017) The influence of creative mindsets on achievement goals, enjoyment, creative self-efficacy and performance among business students, *Thinking Skills and Creativity*, **24**, pp. 1–11, https://doi.org/10.1016/j.tsc.2017.02.007 (archived at https://perma.cc/GMU2-KGQS)

Rees, A et al (2017) The impact of breaks on sustained attention in a simulated, semi-automated train control task, *Applied Cognitive Psychology*, **31** (3), pp. 351–59, https://doi.org/10.1002/acp.3334 (archived at https://perma.cc/ELH9-A7CA)

Sonnentag, S (2012) Psychological detachment from work during leisure time, *Current Directions in Psychological Science*, **21** (2), pp. 114–18, https://doi.org/10.1177/0963721411434979 (archived at https://perma.cc/2YP3-3D93)

SPARK (2017) The Impact of Absenteeism, SPARK Blog, ADP, http://www.adp.com/spark/articles/2017/01/the-impact-of-absenteeism.aspx (archived at https://perma.cc/ADR5-BS5G)

Williams, M E (2021) The dangers of overtaxing your prefrontal cortex, *Salon*, www.salon.com/2021/12/12/the-dangers-of-overtaxing-your-prefrontal-cortex/ (archived at https://perma.cc/2YP3-3D93)

Yup, K (2022) 'How people fall apart': Yale faculty discuss the impact of burnout on the brain, *Yale Daily News*, https://yaledailynews.com/blog/2022/03/29/how-people-fall-apart-yale-faculty-discuss-the-impact-of-burnout-on-the-brain/ (archived at https://perma.cc/AC9D-VCH2)

Chapter 6: Reconnect with your curious mind!

Blue, J (2022) The role of curiosity in learner engagement, World of Better Learning, Cambridge University Press, www.cambridge.org/elt/blog/2022/02/22/engine-achievement-role-curiosity-learner-engagement/ (archived at https://perma.cc/54XX-S8F7)

Cambridge Dictionary (2019) Originality, https://dictionary.cambridge.org/dictionary/english/originality (archived at https://perma.cc/F4QX-P5XP)

Crawford, L (2022) The Default Mode Network (DMN), o8t, www.o8t.com/blog/default-mode-network (archived at https://perma.cc/9F6W-TRKK)

Farnham Street (2014) Steve Jobs on Creativity, https://fs.blog/steve-jobs-on-creativity (archived at https://perma.cc/W98N-2VJN)

Fohtung, J (2016) The evolution of the concept of creativity, LinkedIn, www.linkedin.com/pulse/evolution-concept-creativity-jacob-fohtung/ (archived at https://perma.cc/2A2G-V4ZF)

Mcleod, S (2009) Unconscious Mind, Simply Psychology, www.simplypsychology.org/unconscious-mind.html (archived at https://perma.cc/45Q5-U637)

Weingarten, G (2007) Pearls before breakfast: Can one of the nation's great musicians cut through the fog of a D.C. rush hour? Let's find out, *Washington Post*, www.washingtonpost.com/lifestyle/magazine/pearls-before-breakfast-can-one-of-the-nations-great-musicians-cut-through-the-fog-of-a-dc-rush-hour-lets-find-out/2014/09/23/8a6d46da-4331-11e4-b47c-f5889e061e5f_story.html (archived at https://perma.cc/9JC7-AJSY)

Chapter 7: Productive mind wandering

Bergland, C (2022) Daydreaming helps the brain pick up faint whispers of memory, *Psychology Today*, www.psychologytoday.com/gb/blog/the-athletes-way/202210/daydreaming-helps-the-brain-pick-faint-whispers-memory (archived at https://perma.cc/P537-MLND)

Bigelsen, J and Schupak, C (2011) Compulsive fantasy: Proposed evidence of an under-reported syndrome through a systematic study of 90 self-identified non-normative fantasizers, *Consciousness and Cognition*, **20** (4), pp. 1634–48, https://doi.org/10.1016/j.concog.2011.08.013 (archived at https://perma.cc/S6W2-QJVZ)

Cirino, E (2017) Maladaptive Daydreaming, *Healthline*, www.healthline.com/health/mental-health/maladaptive-daydreaming#symptoms (archived at https://perma.cc/Y88P-2PZ6)

Davis, D M and Hayes, J A (2012) What are the benefits of mindfulness? *American Psychological Association*, **43** (7) http://www.apa.org/monitor/2012/07-08/ce-corner (archived at https://perma.cc/FU25-9JEF)

Fisher, J (2024) Maladaptive daydreaming: What it is and how to stop it, *Harvard Health*, www.health.harvard.edu/mind-and-mood/maladaptive-daydreaming-what-it-is-and-how-to-stop-it (archived at https://perma.cc/J7JE-DFVB)

Neuroscience News (2022) Your mind wanders because your brain whispers, *Neuroscience News*, https://neurosciencenews.com/daydreaming-memory-hippocampus-21669/ (archived at https://perma.cc/C85K-BBLF)

ScienceDaily (2023) What happens in the brain while daydreaming? www.sciencedaily.com/releases/2023/12/231213112457.htm (archived at https://perma.cc/8GFH-JA6C)

Somer, E (2002) Maladaptive daydreaming: A qualitative inquiry, *Journal of Contemporary Psychotherapy*, **32**, https://somer.co.il/articles/2002Malaptdaydr.contemp.psych.pdf (archived at https://perma.cc/6YRF-6GDW)

Somer, E, Lehrfeld, J, Bigelsen, J and Jopp, D S (2016) Development and validation of the Maladaptive Daydreaming Scale (MDS), *Consciousness and Cognition*, **39**, pp. 77–91, https://doi.org/10.1016/j.concog.2015.12.001 (archived at https://perma.cc/76L6-MZ8V)

Summer, J (2021) Maladaptive daydreaming: symptoms and diagnosis, Sleep Foundation, www.sleepfoundation.org/mental-health/maladaptive-daydreaming (archived at https://perma.cc/EKL8-YFPT)

Thurber, J (1939) 'The Secret Life of Walter Mitty', *The New Yorker*, www.newyorker.com/magazine/1939/03/18/the-secret-life-of-walter-mitty-james-thurber (archived at https://perma.cc/56PY-G422)

Chapter 8: Harness the power of focused daydreaming

Scotti, J F (2023) The power of intention for living fully, *Psychology Today*, www.psychologytoday.com/gb/blog/buddhist-psychology-east-meets-west/202303/the-power-of-intention-for-living-fully (archived at https://perma.cc/J9CS-Y85U)

Sun, J et al (2021) The bright side and dark side of daydreaming predict creativity together through brain functional connectivity, *Human Brain Mapping*, **43** (3), pp. 902–14 https://doi.org/10.1002/hbm.25693 (archived at https://perma.cc/Y6P2-FD6M)

Chapter 11: Soaring swans

McKinsey (2021) Building workforce skills at scale, www.mckinsey.com/capabilities/people-and-organizational-performance/our-insights/building-workforce-skills-at-scale-to-thrive-during-and-after-the-covid-19-crisis (archived at https://perma.cc/T2KL-C7R5)

NFER (National Foundation for Educational Research) (nd) The Skills Imperative, www.nfer.ac.uk/key-topics-expertise/education-to-employment/the-skills-imperative-2035/ (archived at https://perma.cc/MT36-DW5F)

OECD (nd) Skills for 2030, www.oecd.org/education/2030-project/teaching-and-learning/learning/skills/Skills_for_2030_concept_note.pdf (archived at https://perma.cc/6JGU-M7ZR)

INDEX

NB: page numbers in *italic* indicate figures or tables

absenteeism, reducing 8, 97
Alternate Uses Test 27
amygdala, the 99, 115–17
anterior cingulate cortex, the 116
anxiety 83, 90
apps, proliferation of 41–42
Archimedes 58
Aristotle 13
Arnsten, Amy 100, 101
Artificial Intelligence (AI) 29, 51–54
　anxiety about 185
　and burnout 53–54
　skills for working with 54,
　　　184–87, 216, 219–21,
　　　22–23
　and techno-insecurity 46–47,
　　　52
assumptions, avoiding 201–04
attentional control, poor 146, 163
Attention Deficit Disorder (ADD)
　102
Attention Deficit Hyperactivity
　Disorder (ADHD) 24,
　26, 102
'attention economy', the 29–32
　defining 30
Autism Spectrum Disorder (ASD)
　24, 27. 102
Ayoa.com 42, 178

basal ganglia, the 99
Bell, Joshua 135
Blakely, Sara 212–13
boredom, role of 28–29
boundaries, establishing 190
brainstorming sessions, group
　197–99

Branson, Richard 212
breaks, taking 103–08
　and burnout 106
　daydreaming breaks 110–12
　'micro-breaks' 107–08, 191
　scheduling 87–88, 210
Broca's area 99
Brod, Craig 44
Brontë sisters, the 64–65
Buffett, Warren 212
burnout 47–51, 182, 219
　breaks, taking 106
　causes of 51
　defining 48–49
　and neuroscience 100–01
　signs of 113–17
Busy Fool Syndrome (BFS) 3, 11,
　32, 156, 160
　and burnout 47, 54, 96, 101–02
　co-dependence with 157
　escaping 181–94, 225
　　Artificial Intelligence (AI),
　　　utilizing 184–87
　　company culture, changing
　　　192
　　'micro-breaks' 191
　　mindset, changing your
　　　184, 192–93
　　'no', saying 189–90
　　and neurodivergence (ND)
　　　25–26
　　and productivity 86, 87
　　symptoms of 5
　　'why?', asking 127, 130

Chambers, Anna 147–48
chores, doing 174–75, 176–77

Christie, Agatha 65
comfort zone, your 132–33
commute time, your 12, 28, 177
conscious mind, the 120, 121
'content', proliferation of 124
convergent thinking 27
creativity, as a skill 21–23
cynicism 49

Davis, Josh 111
Davis, Paula 49
daydreaming 23, 58–71
    and art 62–65
    attentional control, poor 146,
        163
    benefits of 17, 71
    and boredom 29
    brain activity during 19, 183
    breaks for 110–12
    and childhood 77–80
    and connectivity 84
    cultural associations with
        17–18
    defining 15–18
    and emotional wellbeing 70
    functions for 16–17
    and guilt 157–59
    guilty-dysphoric 146
    and innovation 65–67
    maladaptive 141, 143–47, 161
        and dissociation 145–46
        defining 143
        symptoms of 144
    and music 68
    myths vs facts 92–93
    as a natural process 69–70
    negative views of 75–76
    and neurodivergence (ND)
        26–27
    and neuroplasticity 79–80
    and overthinking 88–91, 132,
        153
    and productivity 84–88, 97
    prompts for 84

and revelations 68
and space travel 60–62
vs worrying 82–83, 153
as a waste of time 182
    see also 'focused daydreaming'
devices, use of 28, 30–31, 37, 38,
    76, 85
discernment 140
dissociation 145–46
dyscalculia 102
dyslexia 25, 102, 103
dyspraxia 102

Edison, Thomas 66, 67
Einstein, Albert 67
emails, work 2, 28
    'techno-invasion' 45, 50
evaluation apprehension 197
executive function 99, 100

fear of failure 81
feng shui 125
'focused daydreaming' 13, 32–34,
    57–58, 183–84
    benefits of 70–71, 183
    dedication to 138
    fostering at work 209–13
        breaks, scheduling 210
        daydreaming workshops
            211
        storytelling culture 211
    and future job skills 219–20
    in the right state, getting
        160–61, 172–79
        activities for 174–79
    in your regular routine 159,
        187–89
    inspiration, information for
        168–72
    intentions, setting 164–68
    and memory 141, 147–51
        hippocampus, role of the
            148–49
    process of 33–34

vs maladaptive daydreaming 141, 143–47, 161
Ford, Henry 200
Fox, Douglas 74
Freudenberger, Herbert 114
Freud, Sigmund 120–21
frontal cortex, the 99, 100, 116
'frontal fatigue' 101–02
frontal lobe 11

Gates, Bill 212
Goddard, Robert 60–62
'group think' 197
guilty-dysphoric daydreaming 146

Helton, William 104–05
hippocampus, the 99, 148–49
Hopper, Edward 65
hours worked vs productivity 96–97
'how-to' approach 200
Huffington, Arianna 113
'hyper-focus' 102

idea generation, group 197–99
insomnia 106
intentions, setting 164–68

Jobs, Steve 123

Kahneman, Daniel 39
karma 165
Kekulé, August 68

Land, George 78
limbic system 116, 126

maladaptive daydreaming 143–47, 153, 161
Matisse, Henri 65
meditation 151–52, 153
meetings, aimless 5, 6
meta-cognition 216–18, 219, 221
'micro-breaks' 107–08, 191

micro-habits 188–89
mindfulness 130–31, 151–54
mind maps 177–78, 191
mindset, importance of 9–10, 184, 192–93
morale, employee 49
Mozart, Wolfgang 68
Mullis, Kary 68
'multi-app overload' 41–42
multitasking 5, 177
music, listening to 178
Musk, Elon 213

neurodivergence (ND) 24–27, 102–03
neurodiversity 102
neuroplasticity 79–80, 88, 101, 127
neuroscience 98–102
    amygdala, the 99, 115–17
    anterior cingulate cortex, the 116
    basal ganglia, the 99
    brain activity during daydreaming 183
    and burnout 100–01, 114–16
    frontal cortex, the 99, 100, 116
    'frontal fatigue' 101–02
    frontal lobe 11
    hippocampus, the 99, 148–49
    limbic system 116, 126
    occipital cortex, the 99
    parietal lobe, the 99
    temporal lobes, the 99
    thalamocortical circuits, the 148–49
Newport, Cal 43
Newton, Issac 18, 68
'no', saying 189–90

Obsessive-Compulsive Disorder (OCD) 24
occipital cortex, the 99
originality, defining 122–23

parietal lobe, the 99
perfectionism 81
perspectives, different 204–06
Picasso, Pablo 201
procrastination 32, 85, 88, 158
production blocking 197
productivity, vs busyness 3
Proust, Marcel 204

'quiet quitting' 6

reframing 199–201
Rego, Mark 101
remote working 5–6
'representational drift' 79
reverse brainstorming 206–09
    steps to 208
rumination 106

'Secret Life of Walter Mitty, The'
    142–43
self-talk, negative 158
serotonin 23
shower, ideas in the 21
silence 178
Simon, Herbert 30
Singer, Judy 25
'Slow Productivity' 43
social loafing 197
social media 2, 28, 51, 108, 179
Somer, Eli 145
Sonnentag, Sabine 106–07
spider diagrams 177–78, 191
status quo, challenging the
    201–04
Steinem, Gloria 134

subconscious mind, the 120–21,
    122, 123–24, 142, 149
    fuelling 125–27
    inspiration, information for
        168–72
    'why?', asking 128
System 1 vs System 2 thinking
    39–40
Szilard, Leo 68

task switching 42
'technostress' 44–47
    techno-complexity 45–46
    techno-insecurity 46–47
    techno-invasion 45
    techno-overload 45
    Technostress 44
    techno-uncertainty 46
temporal lobes, the 99
thalamocortical circuits, the
    148–49
Thinking, Fast and Slow 39
Thurber, James 142–43
'tortured artist fallacy', the 62–65

unconscious mind, the 121
upskilling 46

Vervaeke, Koen 148
visualization, positive 171
Visuri, Ingela 26

Wernicke's area 99
'what if?' scenarios 176
'why?', asking 127–30
worrying 82–83, 153, 176

Looking for another book?

Explore our award-winning books from global business experts in Skills and Careers

Scan the code to browse

www.koganpage.com/sce

Also from Kogan Page

ISBN: 9781398607064

ISBN: 9781398607941

ISBN: 9781398604841

ISBN: 9781398613294

www.koganpage.com